I0449877

Mormon is Global

AA BASTIAN

Preface & Acknowledgements

The spark lit in the first edition began burning for a second. Thanks to colleagues, friends and family for feedback that nuances and enlivens this new edition. I still do not consider this a definitive volume but an evolving process to disguss an intricate global network of Mormons while acknowledging challenges and obstacles.

You'll notice that nearly every page is updated. Whole new sections have been added. Dialogue is not in quotation marks because it approximates real conversations but are not directly word for word.

I want to particularly thank Dr. Staci Ford at the University of Hong Kong and the readers, historians, church officials, and publisher I met through her for revealing holes in the first edition to me. Staci encouraged me to refine my discussion of race. I appreciate Allen and Jill Anderson for encouraging me to continue to write.

I also appreciate my friend Nellene Stevens for making suggestions to the book. Thanks to David Fletcher for contributing thoughts that helped me with this new edition. Thanks to Russell Stevenson for answering many questions. Thanks to Tosawan Malabuppha who traveled with me through Asia and helped open doors to new contacts there. Thanks to the deaf Mormons in Bangalaru, India for hosting us and giving us a window into their lives.

And a special thanks to my mom, Helen Horton, for hours of editing and rigorous debate.

I hope you enjoy.

Introduction

The problem with associating Mormonism and Americanism is that people expect Mormons to behave like Americans. Of course viewing Mormonism in the context of the United States and its influences upon Mormonism is valid and enlightening. While researching in the British Library recently I passed Patrick Hughes' optical illusionary book shelves, entitled *Paradoxymoron* hanging on the wall exemplifying his invention of 'reverspectives' where what is nearest to you appears furthest away. Viewing *Paradoxymoron* from new angles allowed it to morph and move.

Scholars of Mormonism study America and its influences particularly under the umbrella of Christianity which limit legitimate comparisons to other religious theories and ideas. Perhaps, though, like Hughe's 'reverspectives' illusion, what seems furthest away is actually closest to us and vice versa. What if our understanding of Mormonism as American is actually an optical illusion?

Let's begin a new thread in the discussion of Global Mormonism. This book is not meant as definitive but an exploratory spark for further inquiry ideally followed up by rigorous data analysis. For now, however, I'd like to hypothesize a counter narrative to what many believe is nearly undebateable for Mormon and non-Mormon alike, Mormonism is American.

At ten years-old I rediscovered the United States. My memory until then only consisted of Okinawa, Japan. Too young to remember the years before Japan in New York or California and especially not Oklahoma, I awoke nights from withdrawls in my new home in Provo, Utah missing Okinawa.

Japanese Mormons filled the same social spaces I did. My dad spoke fluent Japanese. It never occurred to me that Mormonism was particularly "American" until recently interfacing with Mormon scholars. While I listened to the arguments and understood the premices, my own experience with Mormonism conflicts with that 'American' story. After years of slushing around in my head, I attempt to lay out the multi-colored glass pieces I've encountered in Mormonism to test them in new dimensions, not to replace the mosaic but rediscover it from a new angle using an international lens.

Graduate school in England completely revolutionized my understanding of who I am as a

Mormon. I studied International Law and World Order at The University of Reading in England. When we got to the American centric International Relations theories, our professors threw out the driest of bones or a curt 'we'll-skip-that-discussion-for-now' and then moved on. So although I'm American, I'm not the expert on American centric theories or ideas. Turning that page with barely a glance, one of the more ingrained lessons of grad school was that the United States actually exists for vacations, Coca-Cola, invention of slang, and entertainment media. I also learned that while the world expresses frustration over US policies, most don't understand the domestic constraints that lead to those policies.

Another ah-ha moment occurred in a van on the outskirts of Reading. An English Mormon family adopted me aiming to enculturate me by wheeling me around their favorite haunts and explaining old-time traditions. Sometime mid-excursion on a lush tree lined road they related the British tradition of Roadshows, something I participated in growing up as a Mormon in Japan and the US. I mentally rolled my eyes thinking, this and other sites they were showing me wasn't British, this is Mormon. Then my eyes widened. British *is* Mormon or Mormon is British, at least the Mormon I am.

Back home in her cumfy sofa chair in Provo, Utah my grandma spilled to me what she'd probably been trying to tell me my whole life. She is British. British immigrats in Utah congregated in Springville where she was born and grew up. Since the 1840s and 50s, having only slight exposure to the outside world, her family almost froze the British culture with which they arrived. Other immigrant communities similarly kept their traditions predating their conversion to Mormonism.

Lastly, Mormons judiciously kept a promise to the state of Israel to refraim from procelyting within its borders. I learned that there are times and places when setting religion aside fosters a neutral space for mutual understanding. Because my grandpa directed Brigham Young University's satellite center in Jerusalem, his leadership personally influenced how I view Mormon international diplomacy.

Therefore, this book is not a discussion of religious tenants but an exploration of the social dynamics of Mormonism. I'll leave doctrines for religious scholars and practicioners to analyze. Religious concepts are referenced only to illuminate their social implications. I also translate Mormon internal verbage for a wider audience.

This work intends to reconcile my long time encounter with Asia, my family's strong relationship with Israeli-Palestinian dynamics, my International Relations postgraduate work in the United Kingdom, and my own Mormonness which first buds in the 1830s-50s.

Mormon Vassal State

What if we assess the social affairs of Mormonism in terms of International Relations? Let's question the assumption that Mormons in Utah are among the most American of Americans. Imagine instead Mormons as a vassal state ('state' would be roughly equivalent to a country as in a nation-state) subject primarily to the United States government with satelites with porous borders subject to governments around the world. Political variables within this vassal state coexist with the larger non-Mormon host government but vary in the way decisions are made and executed. Roughly this is like renting a bike in a city. You're free to zoom around town but you are expected to maintain certain rules. Freedom of religion under the US constitution allows relatively free governance to Mormons but as a vassal it is still required to maintain certain rules and norms.

Outside of our normal conceptions of Mormons that center or respond to Mormons in Utah, Idaho, Arizona, and Wyoming let's adjust our microscope. Might we see a new slice of the organism?

The Vassal State

Section One

Mormon Utah

Bouncing thin carrot curls spliced into the gene pool from my Irish grandmother several greats ago. Leaving Ireland and the enduring effects of the potato famine she boarded a ship in Liverpool with the Mormons. In the British immigrant town of Springville, Utah she lived in a small hastily built house in the backyard of her husband and his first wife. Grandma, who knew my Irish grandmother's children and grandchildren, attested to her grattitude for what she had in Utah, a house, husband, land and children she never would have attained in Ireland.

Britons neighbored her on all sides, many from northern England. Britons lived in towns scattered throughout Utah. Further south iron workers straight from the mines and factories of northern England resumed their skills in Iron County, Utah.

Scandinavian Mormons lived in pockets throughout the territory as the second largest immigrant population. Karl G. Maeser, a German-Mormon immigrant founded Brigham Young University in a town called Provo. German is now the third most spoken language in Utah. Even a substantial population of Polynesians settled a town forty miles southwest of Salt Lake City they named Iosepa, or Joseph. Though most of them returned to Hawaii in the early 20th century.

Amidst the thousands of multi-national immigrants in the 1850s it is curious why the Mormon prophet and apostles, the top fifteen leaders of that generation, either were all or mostly all American-born converts. How would apostles comprehend the traumas of the potato famine to minister appropriately to an Irish woman without a British-born, or perhaps more particularly, an Irish-born convert in their quorum advising them? Britons of the day didn't seem too concerned, nor did the Germans or Scandinavians or other Europeans. No mass protests, no mass dissatisfaction occurred over an American-born leadership.

Perhaps my Irish grandmother and her associates were too uneducated and too dependent on Americans to worry over representation in the hierarchy's top eschelons. Perhaps Britons in Springville preferred their lifestyle nearly unchanged culturally from the Liverpool area and preferred concentrating on their own community. Ascending to upper management meant long hours, inter-cultural dilemmas, and fending off taunting from US government and other hostile non-Mormon Americans.

Clinging to their British culture appears to have been a higher priority than representative leadership. Whether by choice or opportunity they intermarried with other Euro-born converts and their descendents. Many American-born converts and their descendents inter-married amongst themselves as well.

Instead of the rich immigration depot of Utah in the 1850s, people world-wide imagine Mormons today as men in overalls and women in bonnets crossing the plains; persecuted religious Americans moving west. Mormon leaders themselves, in their attempt to portray Mormons in a certain way, allowed certain types of people and culture to model Mormonism to the world but not other cultures. That image reinforces the idea that Mormons are American, and of course many are, now. The Mormon Trail delivered pioneers, a mosiac of one of the great stories of westward expansion to the frontiers, and most were not Americans. Not only were they not Americans, they originally used an entirely separate coinage system, policing system and government from the United States in Utah. Federal minders linked Utah Territory only loosely to the rest of America.

Mormon converts, beginning in the early to mid-nineteenth century, didn't only join the church they were expected to drop everything and emigrate to 'America' which was actually Utah. This is similar to someone receiving a lucrative job offer contingent upon a permanent relocation to Dubai. It's this notion of emigration reaching beyond religion; touching on citizenship, patriotism, loyalites, economics, and social networks.

If you talk to historians in England, they'll tell you that British-born Mormons far exceeded the number of American-born Mormons. In the first one hundred years, for example, at least half of British-born converts or at least 50,000 and up to 100,000 emigrated to Utah. Compare that to the estimated 12,000 American-born converts who originally migrated to Utah. That's at least a ratio of 1 to 5. Many of the Britons inherited generations of poverty, a sizeable number with little education. Americans that migrated to Utah also lived in poverty, though not all Britons or Americans came from generational poverty. Some Americans had been temporarily displaced from the economy by the Revolutionary War and the War of 1812 that ravaged New England.

Many of the American-born Mormons also descended from British ancestry. Combining American-born and British-born converts in Utah heavily Anglo-sized the approach to Mormonism. Scandinavians, Germans, Polynesians, and others had to contend with an overwhelmingly British influenced culture and language. And remember, Britons in the 1850s were at the height of their civilizing mission to the world. In fact, when the city of Provo in Utah earned a reputation for rebelliousness, a select number of families moved into town to civilize them, a very British-Euro mentality of the day. Perhaps a more accurate explanation was an infiltration to make sure the folks in Provo learned the proper way to behave according to British standards of gentility.

Both sides of my family are primarily British with other European-born immigrants and their descendents, Mormon since the 1830s-50s. There are only a very few American-born converts among these ancestors. The question arises, how European is Utah? Does the term 'American' actually mislead the wider public? Should we refer to Utah as an international migration depot or a mini-British/Euro-American enclave with Polynesians set amidst a backdrop of Native Americans and their land? These immigrants and their American advisors settled together among Native Americans nestled against the steep Rocky Mountains to the east, slowing intercourse with most of the continental United States for at least a century. Unlike traders, merchants, and gold diggers from the east on their way to California or the Northwest Territories who actually were Americans, the Mormons of Utah enticed and tried to welcome anyone who would come, American or not. Britons and Europeans flowed to Utah in a river and other peoples like my Armenian ancestor dribbled into the Mormon territory.

Learning to survive off the land required new skills the majority of Britons had not yet acquired in the developed economy of northern England. Leaving neighborhoods in England where families knew each other for centuries to restart in Utah with foreign, even strange British neighbors, necessitated a new fortress of trust. Americans were even more foreign despite their British ancestral pedigree, especially non-Mormon Americans among whom they had little exposure except through newspapers and textbooks. Germans, Scandavians, and Polynesians met new neighbors in their towns and had to learn English to coexist with the large British, and sometimes unaccomodating, presence.

Grandma, from her sofa chair told me of her forebearers' fear of Native Americans who carried out seemingly random theft. Apparently, though my grandma might have rosified the story, Native Americans liked one of my great grandmothers because she braved interactions with Native Americans leaving plates of food outside for them. Life had been untenable in poverty-stricken Ireland and northern England but Native Americans didn't want them in Utah. Tensions between the new settlers and those who'd been living on the land for centuries sometimes led to violence. Not all Mormons encouraged interaction and acceptance of Native Americans. Some, though, did become Mormons of their own choosing. Americans on the east coast disdained Mormons but luckily American authorities in Great Salt Lake, as the capital city was known, handled diplomacy with the US government.

Waving American flags served more than patriotism. Gratitude for their new lives partially did motivate them. Proving to US federal officers sent from the east coast to monitor Mormons, that they were loyal citizens might have also been a strong motivation. However, while we know of a significant Euro and specifically British-born population in Utah, the actual numbers and influence from British-born Mormons may be slanted in popular memory for several reasons.

Downplaying the numbers and portrayals of foreign-born Mormon immigrants to federal officials and to the outside non-Mormon world, might have been unintentional. A heavy percentage of foreign-born women converted, for example, whose stories Mormon histories have not emphasized until recently. Perhaps focusing on the male population of Mormons as representing families, unintentionally skewed the international nature of the population. Women, after all, incubate the culture of a nation and heavily influence even their American-born husbands and children. These international stories are not known as such.

Escaping poverty in northern England to travel to the United States was dangerous and expensive. Mormons offered a much safer route out of northern England with a network at every stop along the way. When women arrived in Utah, because of polygamy, anyone who wanted could be married. Excess wives avoided census counts to protect their husbands from jail skewing actual counts of foreign-born converts in Utah. A Mormon historian counting men as heads of households, and who may also have incentive to avoid a discussion on polygamy, might wildly misrepresent the international character and diversity of Mormon Utah. Census data may misrepresent the British-Euro character of the community.

Another consideration for the statistics of foreign to American-born immigrants in Utah may be difficult to actuate because American-born converts bore a lot of children, perhaps even more on average than other groups in Utah. This might have inflated over generations the numbers of American-born and their descendents through polygamy. This would require a count to compare the numbers, though some of these numbers may be difficult to nail down acurately.

Returning home to extended family on the east coast and mid-west was far easier for Americans who decided to quit the harsh frontier life. Europeans may not, on average, have had as many children as Americans but they continued to trickle in from Europe until the mid 20th Century and had a more difficult time returning home once they got there. Not to mention, how would a European know the difference between the America in the east and mid-west of the United States and the 'America' of Utah? Many of them landed in New Orleans completely missing everything east of the Mississippi River. Therefore, census data might not accurately reflect how European Mormon Utah became because American and foreign-born converts were not static or all accounted for. Nor might Europeans be fully aware of themselves in comparison to other developed immigrant experiences in the United States.

Masking the influence and strength of the British and European as well as the other non-American populations' numbers may also have been intentional. Mormon leaders settled American-born converts closer to Great Salt Lake where federal minders might concentrate and confirm Mormons' 'Americanness'. They settled foreign-born converts, like my Irish grandmother, further south sprinkled amongst Americans. Springville, for example, is over an hour's drive from Salt Lake City. A horse would take at least twelve hours on the same route.

Now imagine the American-born converts who migrated to Utah. They came from a specific time frame and culture in American history. American-born converts who matured into adults in New England before they became Mormon grew up with the diversity of the first waves of non-British immigration, Germans and Italians. Black populations leaving the horrors of slavery were still relatively small, though growing. Americans in the United States didn't witness diversity of immigration and emancipation of the enslaved populations until after American-born Mormons had almost disappeared behind the mountains in the deserts of Utah. Americans in California, and the east coast cities of New York, Washington DC, Philadelphia, then Chicago, Detroit, and Miami meshed out intercultural and inter-racial conflicts independently of Mormons in Utah. They both, Mormons in Utah and Americans outside of Utah, encountered a singular variety of diversity at a different pacing. Both societies found unique ways of confronting it.

Also, remember American-born descendents of Britons in or from New England viewed England's institutions and culture differently than British-born Mormon immigrants to Utah. During that early era in the 1830s-50s, American-born British still had grandparents who served or were economically displaced by the American Revolutionary War or the War of 1812 against Britain. New Englanders came to view their ancestral British fathers as tyrannical enemies. In 1830 and beyond, though, British-born Mormons found refuge in the United States and were happy to call themselves 'American' without the same degree of antagonism or aspiration for a separate American identity than a New Englander of British descent carried. Britons in the 1850s sought an economic edge in America rather than necessarily an escape from tyranny.

American views in regard to diversity evolved separately from Mormons in Utah: American, British, European, or any other immigrants. Two distinct modes of managing diversity developed independently. There are instances of course where Mormons and Americans interacted but perhaps only on the scale a vassal state would interacting with its host nation. Much of 'American' history marched forward without Mormons. They were and generally are still not included in American history books except their exodus to Utah. American historians like John Bicknell are now integrating these histories of Mormons and other Americans.

Mormons, like my immigrant Irish grandmother in the 1850s, read in newspapers about the changing landscape of the US by the rock of a chair on her porch. For future generations news would come by radio, then later, television. It probably didn't occur to her that the narrative happening in Mormon Utah in front of her became siphoned off from the US and invisible to the rest of 'America'. Of course Britons in Liverpool and elsewhere similarly read articles about the US reprinted in their own newspapers. It seems plausible that although Mormons in Utah may have absorbed more 'Americanness' while in Utah, maybe not much more than their compatriate Britons in England would absorb.

In fact, from a logistical point of view, Utah was just as distant from New York and Washington, DC as Liverpool especially before the railroad. Crossing the Rocky Mountains in a wagon then the plains of the mid-west to travel east could easily be as complicated or even more treacherous than boarding a ship from Liverpool to New York. Let alone the delay that overland or shipping would add to the speed and access of news. Reading about tensions over immigration and racial strife in newspapers must have generated at least some anxiety among British and

European-born Mormons who already knew, or quickly found out, Americans held disdain and even hatred for Mormons. Conscious or even unconscious fears would naturally reading about tensions in the rest of the United States. Reading rather than participating adds ambiguity and a lost sense of control over events which may even have stirred more fear than if they'd been present amidst the tensions on the American east and west coasts themselves.

From 1850 to 1857 Brigham Young served as both Mormon prophet and governor of Utah territory. Mormons revered their prophet and church president similar to a Briton revered his queen. For a hearty British and European population in Utah, a hierarchy who ruled until their death with a recognized successor must have been a welcome comfort, obvious, unquestioned and an echoing of their origins. Polynesians and other royalty oriented cultures may have felt the same way. And it is interesting to note that every Mormon prophet-president has served his procelyting mission to England except President Thomas S. Monson so far. (President Monson didn't serve a Mormon mission.)

Thus Mormondom after the 1850's was not predominantly American. This Mormon vassal state expanded within Utah and surrounding states until bloated. Then in the 1950's with emerging airplane and under-ocean telephone cables Mormon leaders encouraged global satellite locations, or mini vassal states. These mini vassal states, called 'stakes' and 'regions', must adhere to their own secular governments' legal code then to leaders in Mormon Utah. Leaders in Mormon Utah must ultimately adhere to US law. And so it creeps outward.

The Mormon vassal was even distinct from the federalized state of Utah, created in 1896, nearly fifty years after my Irish grandmother and her British neighbors in Springville had established themselves as what they believed was 'American'. Current issues like why the Mormon top leadership, called the First Presidency and Quorum of the Twelve, continue to preference white Mormons from Utah to lead despite its growing international presence may not be a recent dilemma. It appears that what looked so American may not really have been American at all. Might it be time to respond to these international, intercultural realities?

The East

Karthik Thandavamurthy wouldn't mind signing an autograph, especially for a couple of twinkle under lovely loppy lashes. Karthik is Mormon. He's Indian from Bangalaru. He's Deaf. He also loves working with Mormon missionaries to translate for other deaf Indians interested in learning more about the Mormons.

This is what it looks like. The missionaries, who often are an Indian paired with a non-Indian, take turns sharing parts of the lesson. Karthik, who can't hear a word they're saying and most often doesn't have an interpreter with him, waits until they finish their spiel, then the missionaries gesture or point to the topic and content they just discussed. Karthik knows the lesson inside out and translates it into Indian Sign Language for the interested parties. It's not only brilliant, it's working. He and other deaf Indians have had so much success in bringing their deaf Indian peers into the church that the community has become quite large.

Indians have been joining the Mormons and running their own congregations since at least the 1850s even though they did not emigrate to Utah territory. Indians learned about the Mormons just like their peers in the West, from colleagues and associates, from missionaries, and from gossip buzzing about Mormons just as it did in the United States. For various reasons over the years Indian Mormons have melted into the larger Indian population but now recently resurged. But they've always been interested in Mormonism.

A common critique of Indian conversions, or even Asian and non-Christian conversions in general, has been that they convert by coersion or for much needed food, education or medical care, not for sincere belief. The phrase people use is "rice-bowl" Chrisians. But Mormons have never, not even in the 1850s, offered food, education, or medical care for joining their group. Non-Indian Mormons ranged from working class farmers and artisans to highly placed British civilians and officers. Indians who joined the Mormons echoed this range of class status, from poor itinerant farmers to upper class Brahmins. In fact, Indians, upon becoming Mormon, ran their own congregations and must have paid at least a tenth of their earnings to be full fledged Mormon members. Indians still became Mormons knowing they wouldn't receive anything from Mormon missionaries who did not bring money with them to India or intended to stay in the first place. On top of that they dealt with much of the same criticism and persecution as their counterparts in Utah territory did.

Karthik would like Mormons to build a temple in India. In a land of temples, it actually seems odd Mormons in Salt Lake would even hestitate. A temple is raised for all sorts of other religious sects and dieties in India. Temples are such a commonality that waiting for a temple until officials in Salt Lake determine their readiness barely makes sense and Karthik's eyebrows will scrunch in response. Yet, so it is.

Temples are actually a peculiarity to Mormons in the United States. While churches dot the corners of many American, British and European streets, temples are rare and to many Westerners, strange. Polygamy is heresy and outlawed in the West but many Mormons with ancestry in Utah and many Asians share polygamist ancestors. A dedicated road to becoming perfect as a new enlightened being equivalent to a type of diety is enough to label Mormons heathen in some circles. But all of these ideas and principles have been or are quite normal and natural in various parts of the East.

In fact, there is a long history of Mormons trying to convince their neighbors that they are actually Christian despite a history of allowing 'heathen' ideas into their canon. Mormons are

Christian and have always been Christian but they do actually seem to share a lot of religious ideas with Asia and other parts of the world as well.

It's almost like a book with two adjoining pages stuck together. When you try to pull the pages apart, some of the story stays stuck to the other sides of the page. Only when you close the book together again are the pages in true sync. In global religion, should some of the story be Christian but other parts be Asian or Eastern? When the right combination of East and West meets together, would we see a coherant whole?

Let's try another analogy. When you're playing futbol, or soccer for the Americans, there's a center line. Two teams stand at various points apart from the center line facing each other. Even if each individual player is relatively closer or further from the center each team is equally distant as a whole from it. A Western Christian society might say that Eastern society is distant from them and so might an Eastern Buddhist or Hindu think Western Christians are distant from them. But they might be just as equally distant away from a center line as the other team.

Is Mormonism a hybrid of both Eastern and Western religious thought currents and therefore close, if not straddling, a center line? A person in the East and in the West might be equally as distant from Mormonism when they are among their non-Mormon societies. Or their societies would see Mormonism equally as strange, equally as normal, or a combination of strange and normal. Perhaps some individuals may be further from the center line than others but as a whole, each side, East and West, is equidistant from that center line. Mormonism demonstrates the possibilities of that kind of hybridity quite well. Detractors have often used the hybridity between Western and Eastern traditions as a point for disdain since the beginning. Africans, Eastern Europeans and Russians must also have currents within Mormonism or be equidistant away from Mormonism since those countries and cultures heavily influence and are influenced by East and West as well.

But talented religious scholars of Mormonism have already carefully traced its influences and thought currents through Western religious theory and practice. No scholar I've met says that Joseph Smith ever met Confucious in a dream. No one says, for example, that Joseph picked up the *Analects* when he was four years old, touching a chord that resurged later in his religious life. So for a moment it looks like Western scholars have pinned it down; Mormonism *is* Western and Christian. No analogies of books with their pages stuck together. No cool futbol team where East and West are as equidistant from a center line of Mormonism. It's all wishful thinking.

And yet.

Western religious thought and philosophy has had a particular penchant for a superiority complex throughout the ages particularly in the 19th Century when Mormonism entered the stage, not to say that any other part of the world hasn't had its own religious or philosophical superiority complexes. It would not be too far of a stretch to say that at least some Eastern ideas and beliefs have seeped into Western thought without attribution, and perhaps more than the West might like to admit. Mormons might say that because diety rules over all the earth he would reveal to each of them parts of his grand vision; that all societies have some truth. But let's take the religious part of this story out so we can look at how East and West might influence each other enough to produce a Joseph Smith with a penchant for religious practices that aligned somewhat with Eastern practices and ideals.

There are two ways Eastern thought has seeped into the West, then I'll tell a story. The first way is through trading relationships with the Levant region stretching across modern day Iran, Iraq, Syria, Lebanon, and Israel/Palestine. Egypt has been a port of major exchange with

Israel/Palestine as well. Trade, and labor exchanges brought ideas from the continents of Africa and Asia into contact with the peoples of Israel/Palestine which developed into a Judeo-Christian ethos. Sure many of those ideas evolved and changed over time to become quite distinct from Asian and African philosophies but elements of those traditions did influence Judeo-Christianity.

The second way Asian and African influence seeped into Western thought came much later during the Age of Sail when Europeans hungered for a little flavor in their diet. Spices from the East drove an engine of explorers who depended on inventors to reach further and more precicely to the edges of the earth. First the Portuguese then the Dutch, and then the British went East. Queen Elizabeth I signed a charter in 1600 for an innovative new company to compete with other Europeans for a slice of that market. Heaven knows a British diet of meat and potatoes could use a crack of pepper and a dash other spices to dress it up, let alone for palatability.

Two hundred and thirty years later when Joseph Smith began curating a complex social and religious project, the young lad whose ancestors were Britons, carried in their DNA Eastern influence, whether they recognized it or not. If a selection of words stemmed from Britain's long association with South, Southeast, East Asia and Africa, like 'peon', 'brain washing', 'guru', 'jungle', 'cushy', 'karma', 'pundit', and 'shampoo', how much more might Eastern ideas have 'brain washed' the thought, architecture and religion of the West? That Joseph Smith might have been naturally inclined to ideas outside his immediate Western sphere is not completely unaccounted for. Even without reference to diety's abilities or inabilities to enlighten a mind, this infusion from the East makes common secular sense.

Acknowledgement of a flow from east to west is important to people. My Bangkok Mormon friend, Tosawan Malabuppha and I traveled to Myanmar recently. Our guide there illuminated not only the history but the religious significance of the pagodas we entered. He pointed underneath one of the ancient pagodas toward an alcove. The soft light and stone shadows arrested my imagination slowing my pace a step.

Doesn't that remind you of windows in the cathedrals of Europe, he said?

And yes, they did. The stone windows curved downward from a point at the top to an open flat ledge. Thick walls gave the window perspective, slanting the light drafting through the hall just like a cathedral.

38

He said the pagoda had been around for centuries, something I expected him to say; but not the next thing he said.

Do you think we got the shape of these windows from the West or do you think this shape just spontaneously appeared on two different hemispheres? Or do you think it's possible that we invented this shape of window first and the West borrowed it from us. Marco Polo traveled through here and so did other Western explorers.

It's possible. What if the inspiration for the shape of cathedral windows did come from the awe inspiring pagodas of Myanmar but was never attributed?

But perhaps an even more important point is that it mattered to this man that not all civilization and beauty is attributable to the West, that perhaps something as sacred and beautiful as a cathedral's window might actually originate in the East.

While looking at each other from West to East and East to West, the other seems far away. But where is the centerline and can it reasonably be said that Mormons occupy that space, each person equidistant from the center though far from each other? And if it appears not, should Mormons move to that center line? Or should own the center line if they do? Karthik seems just as natural of a Mormon as any Western-born Mormon. Temples hold a natural affinity for him.

Conversion

Once upon a time all converts to Mormonism were invited and even expected to immigrate. Physically immigrate.

Wanna be Mormon? Do you see that ship over there? It's leaving for Louisiana. When you get to the other end, just tell them you're Mormon, etc, etc.

Mormons established an immigrating machine, marked, measured, and manned with trails for massive relocation. When you arrived in Utah territory it didn't always matter what skills or language you came with, someone would hand you a shovel.

Here is your plot.

But I don't know how to farm.

You'll learn.

I don't really like farming. I'm a shoe maker.

You hungry?... You can make shoes, too, but later.

Conversion is still an immigration into the vassal state, but more figurative today. Conflating conversion with immigration, then, may be useful especially in relation to the Mormon vassal state because immigration and conversion actually did go hand in hand for many. Stories of immigration are often mythologized as a man or woman leaving behind an impoverished past to find a better life somewhere else. However, reality is far more complicated for immigrants and rarely if ever entails fully leaving behind a past life. As we have seen already, men and women who became Mormons did not actually leave behind their previous lives. They built new lives in a new location that had characteristics of Mormon ideals and constraints but with heavy influence from old lives they knew from before they immigrated, whether they realized it or not.

My grandmother was Irish and Mormon, a dual identity. She and her English neighbors ate meat and potatoes just like they would've in Britain. Even in the early days men and women carried their old identities and their Mormon identities like a dual passport. They didn't even belong to the United States fully yet. That would happen in fifty years. As we've said, they still belonged to their old lives as well as their Mormon lives and there was really nothing to keep them from being British when all their neighbors were also British. After the 1950s new converts stay in the locations where they live.

Immigration has always been a wrenching, even while packaging crumbles of memory from the past to keep it alive for the journey. Immigration has never been a full separation. No one can replace the years that have passed in their old lives with the new life. Those years are always there informing a person how to walk, how to speak, how to respond to different stimuli, and how to think. Expecting someone to erase those years is futile if not naïve.

And now, when Mormons do not immigrate to Utah any longer, conversion is still an 'immigration' into the vassal state, a wrenching, but it's also still a thrilling, though now more figurative, jump on a ship and grab of the shovel. Becoming Mormon could still take you to places you never dreamed of, even today, at the last moment and without warning. Let's start with the movement any makes philosophically, whether they realize it or not, to the center. Westerners and Easterners and everyone in between adopt values that aproximate each other more closely. Westerners move Eastward. Easterners move Westward and so forth. Then there is a constant churning and negotiation as new converts

43

(immigrants) enter the vassal state. There are certain points that remained fixed but others which constantly open up to or refine new ideas. If Mormons function at a center point, new ideas will assimilate more easily, even if altered slightly.

My roommate in Jerusalem was a convert. Four of us roomed together in Brigham Young University's Jerusalem campus set on a lovely hill overlooking the Old City on the West Bank. She was the first convert with whom I had close interaction. I was eighteen and impressionable. She took it as her mission to open my eyes to the outside world. Mormons, she felt, were too sheltered. She literally grabbed me on her way to adventures speaking with every single human being she could induce to talk to her, partially so that I'd become more exposed.

Truthfully there was a part of me that was slightly offended. I had lived in Okinawa, Japan as a little girl with lots of non-Mormon friends, and not always American either. I lived in Atlanta, Georgia. I grew up with rabbis and Muslims coming to my home. The idea that I was particularly sheltered just because I was Mormon, seemed pretty assumptive. After all, I was in Jerusalem on my own dime. Clearly I valued intercultural understanding and so, probably, did most of the rest of the students on the trip. We were all studying Judaism and Islam; a language,

Hebrew or Arabic; and history of the region. I kept my mouth shut, though, and enjoyed meeting all sorts of new people tagging along by her side. She continued to struggle fitting in as a convert.

One day I asked her what specifically bothered her about being a convert. She rattled off a list of insensitive things people said or did and why those things frustrated her. I listened, but in my head I was thinking, yup, I've done that. Oops, I've said that. Yes, someone's done that to a convert before. Dang, I've been a total jerk to converts in thought and action and didn't even realize.

One of the main frustrations she had was lifer Mormons not valuing her knowledge, skills, and ideas from before she became Mormon. What I didn't realize then but know better now, is that even though both of us were 'American', we came from very different environments. Or perhaps another explanation is that both of us assumed that Mormonism is just a religion, that it's not a different country or society, a vassal state.

Her exposure to a different 'America' than me, made the life and ideas she described to me before she became Mormon, seem a bit foreign. When I'm in Japan, it is clear that I am in a different country and expect cultural diversity. When I'm interacting with a fellow American, I don't expect that same foreignness. I didn't realize at the time just how much different Mormon is from typical American. I thought I was American. Why did she have to be different?

She opened my eyes to the possibility that other Americans are different, or at least more different than I realized. We may watch the same shows and speak the same language but perhaps not have access or affiliate with the same social networks and structures to the same degree. Perhaps I had developed a sort of bilingualism as a Mormon and American, or maybe I wasn't bilingual, yet. Though Americans vary widely and are from various different cultures and races, the concept of a 'melting pot' where certain values and cultural norms are accepted as normal still prevail. We'll talk about some of those later.

There are two major differences between the Mormon vassal state and the United States in regard to entrance, or immigration (conversion). First, the Mormon vassal state and the United States take opposite positions with immigration. Both have toyed with quotas but for opposing goals. The United States employs quotas as maximums to limit the number of immigrants from various countries. The Mormon vassal state sometimes uses quotas as baselines to encourage a minimum number of immigrants. The second difference would be that immigrants to the United

States are often identifiable by accent, knowledge of insitutions, dress, etc. Mormon immigrants carry no identifiable marks and can be virtually invisible as converts. We'll talk about Mormon invisibility in the next section.

For now, imagine chunks of lamb, potatoes and carrots stirred in a pot of warm carmelizing onions. We'll add a sprinkle of cumin, flecks of coriander, a rich curry blend, and a dribble of broth, salted and peppered. Not too much, though. Add spices at just the right potency and your guests crawl back for more. Overwhelm the dish with spices and your guests grin smugly at the exit. This is American immigration. The dish can only integrate so many immigrants before becoming too overwhelmed. Immigrants add flavor at limited quantities the larger body can successfully manage.

But if you own a spice shop, your goals differ considerably. The more spices and the grandest variety you gather for sale, the happier and more diverse your customers. Restaurants of various cuisines, caterers, chefs, concious cooks, markets and sandwhich shops will purchase your spices in greater quantities and variety if only you can gather them to your shop first. This is Mormon immigration. More immigrants means more diversity and richer outcomes for the community as a whole. There is no need to limit quantities because there is infinite space to expand and limitless customers.

Immigration is encouraged, a core value even within the Mormon vassal state. If you aren't engaged in making space for immigrants, you are told that you are not doing your part. And once someone has immigrated, there is no way of knowing, unless they or someone else reveals it that they are in fact immigrants.

Let's start with the implications of the vassal state's core value of immigration. In Mormon terms, this is known as conversion through missionary work, which is actually controversial in some circles. The belief from the outside is that Mormons go around brain washing people into joining their sect to become some sort of automaton of obedience to arbitrary principles that are highly 'American' in nature. Some even compare it to a form of religious colonialism.

If Mormon immigration was actually that horrific or stilting, a lot less people would convert. If it was what outsiders believe it to be, the process may just be the colonial monster garbling away individuality out of the world one Book of Mormon at a time. However, the actual mode and methods of immigration might surprise a few. A dribble of immigration may not create the effect, but massive scale conversion that Mormons integrate since the beginning of their existence actually resists colonialization. Here's why. New waves of immigrants from across the globe force Mormons into constant flux and innovation. Or in other words, continuous immigration instigates a conversion in both directions, to the immigrant and the body into which they are immigrating. First I'll explain how this happens and then tell a story.

When an immigrant arrives in the United States, they present their forms, receive a stamp and a nod, then start making it on their own. Hopefully they have a friend or relative or occupation to feed and house them. Mormons, however, assign people with special care to assist the transition process. A new immigrant enters the Mormon vassal state a little like they would a new country. They meet with visa officers (missionaries) who explain the Mormon vassal state's basic foundation and approve immigrant status. Then a formal citizenship ceremony (baptism) takes place. After that the local Mormon group in which the immigrant lives assigns two to four Mormons to watch out for the new immigrant, temporally and emotionally (or spiritually) as requested or needed. Others will present them lessons and answer questions to smooth integration. New Mormons receive an assignment and start participating in the group quite quickly.

But a process that takes this kind of care in transitioning new immigrants is naturally two-way. That new person becomes so highly engaged in the community that their own personal experiences, life lessons, way of thinking is immediately present and influencing other Mormons in the group, especially the people immediately assigned to assist with their transition. The immigrant often gives a talk to others, may teach a lesson, may organize an activity within weeks of their new citizenship. Other Mormons are now exposed to that person's other citizenship background, their other passport they carried before they became Mormon.

Of course a new immigrant undergoes a wrenching, trying to keep what they loved about their life before, while adopting a new philosophy and life style. Transition into the vassal state can enliven but frighten, too. What the new Mormon may not realize, however, is that because of their immigration, people around them are not stagnant either. In fact, some Mormons thrive on the possibility of learning about another person's background outside of the vassal state. Some Mormons, though, may tire of this constant immigration for the same reason, constant change and integration of people whom they may not share any interests or context. Americans certainly aren't asked to adopt immigrants into their lives every time someone moves from abroad as part of their citizenship requirements. Mormons are invited to do so.

Immigration is exhausting and exhilerating at the same time for both the immigrant and the community who welcomes them. Long time members who've welcomed new immigrants over a life time may work hard to open their homes at first but then hope and expect immigrants take it upon themselves to engage socially on their own merits. Or some long time members don't want to open up to constant change any longer. Some have unrealistic expectations of new immigrants ignoring the rich bilingual, bicultural addition to the community. Bilingual, as in Mormon and some other culture or identity. Dual citizenship. Dual passports. A person never loses membership in the community and nation-state they were born into necessarily. They will always have two passports.

My favorite immigrant/convert perspective story actually comes from London Mormons. I worked as an interpreter in London one summer attending the Mormon congregation on Sundays near Hyde Park. They partitioned off visiting Mormons into a separate class during part of their meeting. The teacher re-educated us, who were mostly American-passport Mormon visitors to London, in Mormon history.

It really goes like this, she instructed. American-born Mormons in the 1830s and 40s nearly lost their minds, as Americans do, seeing wacky visions, sorely mismanaging funds, shaker mentalities, magic rocks, you name it. Essentially American-born Mormons needed straightening and Britons didn't mind taking on the job. Britons infused the Mormons with order and decorum even before they reached Salt Lake City and continued civilizing Americans long afterward. The moral we were to take from the lesson was that when Mormons step out of line, diety sends immigrants to balance and straighten them, in this case, Britons. The very idea that immigrants' influence might be a corrective force for the trajectory of the main Mormon body is real. Immigrants change Mormons and are changed by Mormons at the same time.

It also implies that a person on the outside, who comes from a different background, is as important as an insider to the vassal state, including as a function of keeping Mormons in line and bringing fresh ideas. Porous borders with heavy immigration breathes into Mormons fresh air. Constant immigration into the Mormon vassal state differs from what we think of as American immigration; it's distinctively Mormon. Immigration tries everyone, but it's also dynamic and exhilerating. Massive influx has the potential to overwhelm any original Mormons in a sort of

52

reverse colonialism. Only conversion, missionary work on a large scale, might generate enough new immigrants to dominate the receiving body for reverse colonialism, a trickle of newcomers could be absorbed like spices in a dish, fresh but not overwhelming. Overwhelming the original body of Mormons with immigrants from abroad happened already. At least the British think so; and they're probably right.

Undetected

Short a sign pasted to your forehead that you're a Mormon, there are no clear markers of an immigrant. No way of knowing whether a person has been Mormon for generations or for five minutes. No accent, no specific hair cuts or fashion trends. No jewelry or head gear. And no amount of institutional knowledge or lack thereof readily determines a Mormon. Anyone who believes they can identify a Mormon without that person's self revelation or record number is making an over generalization based on their limited experience with Mormons, even if they happen to be a generational Mormon.

I've heard at least three times in my life that someone 'looks like a Mormon'. Wait what? That is the most perposterous thing I had ever heard. Growing up around Japanese Mormons averted me from imagining Mormons looking a certain way. Oh and then move to Utah where there are a whole lot of rebelious Mormons, you'll see what I mean. These comments refer to a stereotypical Mormon, the images promoted in the past to the exclusion of other looks, but which have never reflected reality as hopefully this book makes the case.

While Mormons may be encouraged to dress modestly, in practice that benchmark slides wildly, especially across countries and cultures, and plenty of Mormons bend that advice. Because there are more Mormons outside of the United States than there are inside, no one can or should intelligently assign a specific cultural or racial look to a Mormon. There are also plenty of people who look and behave just like the stereotyped Mormon but are not. Outward appearance is what each individual Mormon might consider as genteel based on their cultural outlook, or a degree of rebellion against that genteel look. New Mormons do look like Mormons, no matter their background. In Washington DC where there is a large population of Mormons, journalists were shocked during Mitt Romney's campaign to find there were so many Mormons in their midst. Right under their nose.

A certain language barrier may give away a new Mormon at first. Phrases with common meanings in the language don't necessarily hold the same meanings in Mormon usage. Even these phrases, however, don't necessarily peg a recent convert as some people hold on to their own way of speaking long after they've become Mormon. Some lifer Mormons try to use new phraseology to enliven their discourse and new phrases are entering the common usage all the time. Even a lifer Mormon who missed a particular vocabularizing moment might not pick up on that phrase when a new Mormon suddenly uses it. Like what does 'ponderize' really mean anyway? It crept in recently but I may not be using it. Mormons, who are not English speakers, may also not use the English Mormon phraseology either and vice versa. After a few months though, most new Mormons have enough of the vocabulary to sound as Mormon as anyone else.

But surely lack of basic knowledge about Mormons might reveal someone who just became a citizen (baptized) five minutes ago, right? Many immigrants (converts) believe that everyone else knows so much more than they do about being Mormon. They feel left out at times because everyone seems to grasp something they do not. Or Mormons remember a song from their childhood that a new Mormon never learned. Lack of institutional knowledge should surely expose a new Mormon even if their look or phraseology did not.

Yet, because Mormon practice, principles, teachings and songs are in constant change and flux, it is possible for a new Mormon to have more knowledge about present trends than an older more experienced Mormon who doesn't know about a recent change or ignores a new policy or practice. Children's songs change so often that new Mormons may actually hear and learn songs that their longer term Mormon companions do not know. I personally don't know three fourths of the songs I hear Mormon children singing today. Leaders change, policies change, music is composed, mission rules are updated.

Not to mention the amount of lifer Mormons who slept or day dreamed through their religious education courses throughout their maturing years. Their teachers may have been more or less prepared. Access to materials and study texts vary. Manuals today replace lessons taught five years ago. In reality, not knowing a particular point that other people in the room all seem to know means nothing and exposes nothing about a new Mormon. It doesn't mean there isn't a learning curve in adapting to the Mormon vassal state, but what it does mean is that a new Mormon can blend in really easily. Mormons who have been around for a long time sometimes like to go beyond the basics to ask questions and analyze history, but the most interesting of those Mormons will also value a convert's life experience and contributions with a different foundation.

New Mormons can and should feel that 1) their contributions, skills and backgrounds are highly valued even if the man or woman next to them has a 'holier-than-thou' problem (a person who thinks they are more proper because they think they know more). 2) Exposure to outside views is a core value to the general body of Mormons even if those they know personally are frustratingly unable to accept new ideas. 3) New Mormons should never feel that lack of knowledge on a particular point necessarily exposes them as a convert or less intelligent than others in the room. In fact, as times goes on, an immigrant of 30 years will know much more than a generational Mormon of 20 years of age. Flux and alteration are that real among Mormons. Any Mormon who makes another feel less than a full equal has lost the essence of Mormonism; dyanmic, changing, global.

If new Mormons cannot be easily identified, they also can get lost after initial efforts to fellowship them. New Mormons have expressed a sense of betrayal or hypocracy in these instances. At first they are welcomed and then the hospitality wanes. Some interpret this to mean that Mormons only care about the numbers, they've got their convert, now they move on. It's lonely. It's painful.

From a generational Mormon perspective, as we have said, it is nearly impossible to know if someone is new or how new. Or, soon others need attention and concern, too. In a relatively short time, a new Mormon is expected to take on a load of caring for others. One frustrating point for lifer Mormons is when new Mormons don't give back to the community after an initial welcoming phase. Like when you invite a new friend into your circle. At first you don't mind picking him up but over time you expect him to take a turn picking everyone else up, too. Everyone volunteers, cooks meals, cleans up, visits people in need, prepares lessons, talks, and more. Even long term Mormons hope to get involved to meet people. Real friends share interests and experiences. Fellowshippers are only temporary stop gaps in the process of making friends. To be fair to new Mormons, however, there is no guide to steer them through the social aspects of being Mormon. Trial and error certainly roughens the road. Mormons forget, or never knew in the first place, how different the vassal state is for people.

The Mormon corridor running through the American states of Idaho, Wyoming, Utah and Arizona may seem like the opposite of constant change especially in outer areas where folks live in one place all their life. So might rural areas across the globe where people generally move into a neighborhood and stay for life. These groups of Mormons may understandably believe that the people they have lived around their entire lives are the true model of Mormons, that their group represents what all Mormons are or should be.

Dangerous. Later in life they leave their town or move to a new location and may be terribly critical of other Mormons who do not seem to meet arbitrary social standards from where they grew up. They have no way of knowing on an experiential level what it might be like to be Mormon in another neighborhood even down the street. Their own community may have developed certain ways of standardizing who is proper Mormon and who is not. This causes major discrimination and offense to others outside of their neighborhood. Two neighborhoods next to each other might develop totally different Mormon personalities. If a person grows up in that personality their whole life, they may never know that their type of Mormon is not representational of all Mormons. Even I'm surprised at times what people believe is a 'normal' Mormon. Get out more. Mormons are quite diverse, actually.

But constancy and lack of change within some Mormon communities, especially in highly concentrated Mormon areas within Utah, allows for another phenomina. Mormons become the powerful, the popular, the rich, the inventors, the social change makers. They know the top fifteen leaders and their children and spouses personally. They are not a minority within a larger society. They gain a kind of native fluency that grounds the larger vassal state. It's not as new and exciting, it's daily life. They question and push boundaries or hold the foundations so rock steady, you want them to open their mind even just a bit.

New immigrants push the boundaries from the outside merely by their presence, an influx of backgrounds and ideas. Mormons in Mormon rich environments push from the inside, thinking of new ways to solve old problems, bend to fluctuating circumstances, steady the ship, and carry institutional knowledge of years of changes. Some will dynamically change the whole while others will desperately hold on to the past they know and are comfortable with. All sides are vital to keep the clay pot from breaking. Pressure from without and within hold the delecate walls firm, but sometimes too firm.

Mormons may always carry a sense of 'it's time to eat, grab your shovel'. Immigrants are as Mormon as someone born Mormon. Anyone who grabs the shovel and starts digging is welcome and valued even if the constipated, blinded person on the same pew isn't capable of opening up their own life to a new Mormon and their background. If that person doesn't open to immigrants, they don't understand core values in the Mormon vassal state. In the midst of incredible diversity, constant flux and change, a rip tide develops resisting that ever dynamic flow. Creating a common curriculum, developing a common vocabulary and dialogue to rely upon when everything else is moving helps to balance change and constancy.

I'm not sure my roommate from the Jerusalem semester abroad ever felt comfortable as a Mormon. I'm not even sure if she still considers herself as Mormon. But because she immigrated, she touched my life. I met Israelis and Palestinians through her in a way I would not have on my own. She learned enough Mormon to translate for me the world she knew before her baptism. I may be as much changed by her influence, background, and efforts to expose me to new ideas at an impressionable age as she was by immigrating into the Mormon vassal state even if for a short time. My British ancestors didn't fully leave their pasts behind to enter the vassal state. No one does.

Sattelite Vassals

Imagine being a head of state receiving a Mormon leader into your office or reception room to discuss formal recognition. You've heard about the Mormons. Your advisors have researched them diligently. Your country has received humanitarian assistance. Your citizens have taken English lessons from Mormons or received a tuition scholarship to one of their Mormon universities. You've personally met Mormons or your close associates have met them in business meetings and as diplomats for various countries. Now they want a diplomatic relationship including visa entry for their ambassadors (missionaries, public relations representatives, etc).

Imagine now that you've had enough contact with Mormons to know they will keep promises, follow laws, address poverty, and contribute to society. You're ready for the integration process. Two primary areas, hard and soft, now enter into negotiation. Hard areas of negotiation constitute legal integration matters. All Mormon functions within the state must follow all state and local codified laws. Sometimes this process happens after formal recognition as a Mormon within that nation-state tries to do something which is later found to be in conflict with the legal code.

In England, for example, Mormons marry first civally before they marry in Mormon temples. British young men and women by law both must have equal access to youth scouting programs. Americans only send young men. Neither of these policies hold for Mormons in the United States at present. Legal scholars address and resolve incompatible codes. If a conflicting law is known at the outset, either one or both parties withdraw from diplomatic negotiations or strike a compromise. Potentially a regime could negotiate principles affecting the global vassal state. For example, if a regime values a certain family structure and does not accept American ideals of multiple family structures, Mormons may adjust vocabulary and policy to align with the regime's requests to receive formal recognition there.

Then there are soft areas of negotiation. These relate to societal values or norms. For example, the Chinese government issued several points for which Mormons must conform to gain official recognition. One of those had nothing to do with legal code but a social norm. The name of the church, The Church of Jesus Christ of Latter-day Saints as originally translated into Chinese held a dark, end-of-days sentiment, inconsistent with the actual intended meaning. Chinese authorities insisted on an improved translation. And Mormons changed the translation. Other points on the list, however, did not end in compromise. Chinese still do not officially recognize Mormons as a religious entity and both sides are at a draw.

This is roughly similar to moving into a house full of roommates. There is an initial vetting process which may be harder or easier depending on the people and how well they know each other. Then once they decide to live together, there are a few hard areas of negotiation like how the rent will be divided and who will pay utilities. Then there are soft areas of negotiation like who will take out the trash, do the dishes, how to split the fridge. How will disputes be resolved? Each roommate situation will vary depending on the arrangements and the people involved.

So it is with Mormon international relations or any organization, business, or government attempting to establish formal relationships with another entity. From the outside each roommate situation may seem relatively the same but day to day interaction may contrast quite extensively. Mormons in sattelite vassals across the world may seem similar on the outside but are actually under quite different negotiated charters.

Laws are different. Languages are different. Ecosystems are different. Values are different.

If we stopped here, you might imagine a world where Mormons are actually quite unique from each other across the globe with their own individual expressions and expectations as Mormons. From the outside there may seem to be some homogeniety, but there is tremendous variance under the surface. So what unifies a vast network of sattelite vassals with the main vassal in Utah? It's something called "Correlation", highly controversial in some circles.

My grandfather, George Horton, sat in on the original committee that decided to implement the system of correlation. He held a PhD in Curriculum Design. He taught at seminaries and insitutes across the United States and directed the church's international seminary and institute program for a time. These are religious education courses for students ages fourteen to thirty. In his retiring years he spent hours unfolding events to me that led to heavy weight decisions which changed the course of the church's trajectory.

He noticed a problem as he taught religion courses to students, for example. They each brought their own bibles to class with different translations and page numbers. When he'd ask them to turn to a specific passage, it took a long time for everyone to find it in the first place then correlate the various translated versions. Logistics of finding a common denominator with which to discuss soaked up time. A committee was formed to resolve some of these issues and correlation seemed like the right solution. If everyone had a similar base from which to start, Mormons across the globe could communicate more effectively and about higher level topics than just about logistics. In my grandpa's case, all his students would read from the same bible. He'd be able to call out a verse and for those still learning the bible, he could provide a page number. They'd be able to reach the content more efficiently and therefore, cover more information.

My mom remembers grandpa telling a story that is also familiar to my own experiences. At Brigham Young University in Hawaii he taught an introductory course to the Book of Mormon. He rattled off Christian religious phrases like, 'atonement', 'fall', 'Adam and Eve', 'faith'. A student from Asia raised their hand having no idea what those phrases meant. The curriculum assumed a western Christian base of knowledge as a foundation. Increasingly for Mormons, western vocabulary and religious contexts are not the middle ground as a baseline for communication. Asians grasp other Mormon concepts faster than westerners, though. Correlating across east and west, north and south may only make sense from a bird's perspective. At an individual level some Mormons, east and west, north and south, may not understand certain broad currents of change or adjustment.

Teachers, he said, also found that certain topics derailed the course just as much as having everyone bring in their own differing bibles. Everyone brought in their various backgrounds and perspectives and knowledge levels. When certain topics were discussed, the entire class would derail into a complicated discussion and make it challenging to bring everyone onto the same page or continue with the intended lesson. Basic fundamentals would be missed that might have provided a frame work for these more advanced, controversial topics. Curriculum correlation, focuses on basics to provide a foundation for further personal study. It also seemed like a viable solution to cover more topics that had been missed before.

Content management is a common conundrum. Where do you start and stop in the detail you bring to a subject or story? For example, suppose as a curriculum designer you run across this dilemma. A prominant Mormon female leader in history has done enormous work to establish a welfare program for those in poverty in and outside of the vassal state but her husband has an affair and even partially blames it on her. She stays with him anyway. Due to the salaciousness of the affair as well as both of their responses, a student's natural tendency would sidetrack to the affair rather than focus on her monumental achievements assisting those in poverty. Some curriculum developers may choose to leave out the affair for students to value her contribution to the welfare program, allowing them to discover the affair on their own at a later date. Controversy occurs when a student feels cheated, that they have the right to know about the affair. They don't want a person in authority making censoring decisions without their consent.

More recently some blame 'Correlation' for what is wrong with Mormons. In their minds it is a top down brain washing function coming out of a white American system forcing blind obedience. It is like a type of colonialization of practice and thought to subdue individuality and expression among Mormons across the globe. And indeed "Correlation" has morphed and bureaucratized since my grandpa's time to such a degree that for some zealous idealists in the church's office building, even an individual Power Point presentation requires a committee to standardize it. When will the Correlation monstrosity require a committee to be sure you spelled your name correctly? Socialization at its worst is an elite few making too many decisions for the whole.

As we have said, there is incredible diversity across different Mormon sattelites across the globe, at the very least because of their unique laws and values, their dual passport identities, not to mention each individual Mormon's varying hues of expression. But on the other hand there is this mammoth attempt to correlate, socializing everyone into one big standardized whole. A vassal state who has among their core values, the churning force of immigration, is not inherently interested in sameness, right? Yet, in the chaos of unremittant change, correlation seems inevitable as a way to forge constancy.

So why won't Mormons accept correlation as a necessary evil? Many do. Threats of litigation necessitates that all church approved materials run through a correlated system. And for that reason, this book avoids correlation, is not approved by The Church of Jesus Christ of Latter-day Saints, nor does it seek formal approval. I prefer the freedom to think outside the box, test new ideas, move beyond the bureacracy. There are so many materials to correlate in fact, the money, resources and time to correlate them all slows the pace, dampening creativity and innovation.

Yet the problem might not lie with a minimal form of correlation like my grandpa endorsed. The problem may lie with the hero stories that Mormons tell then standardize for the entire global Mormon vassal network. Stories about mostly American-born Mormon converts who crossed plains have gained, through correlation efforts, global hero status because every Mormon in every sattelite studies their lives as models. Perhaps that is alright on some levels but increasing frustration with correlation and 'American' stories make it seem to the global network that only Americans are truly valued within the system.

If we really look at Mormon stories, we find two interesting phenomina. One, almost all Mormon stories begin at or nearly at immigration or conversion. And two, there is very little development of stories before they became Mormon. The most popular Mormon stories are often American-born converts or barely mention the location they came from outside of the United States even when as we have seen, many many foreigners lived in Utah as Mormons. As we mentioned several times in this book, the essence of a Mormon is a dual identity, Mormon and something else. Writers creating stories about Mormons, many times, only emphasize the Mormon aspects of their life, not their past or dueling identities. Because for so long Mormon converts immigrated to Utah, perhaps a subconcious perception developed that converts were only fully Mormon when they became immigrant 'American'. In proper immigrant fashion, the ideal is to 'forget' their past lives; unrealistic and undynamic as the meat for a compelling story.

A legal status as 'American' was an important goal for the entire community especially before Utah became an official US state in 1896. Hero figures that modeled how to be 'American' was a vital part of Mormon integration into the United States as a whole. Stories about Mormons don't actually have to start at or near conversion, nor do models need to come from the United States any longer. From the last 1880s until the 1950s, the centrifuge gradually reversed. Now hero stories can and should come from anywhere within the vast global network of Mormon sattelites. Also, of the current top fifteen leaders of Mormons six were seventeen years of age and older by 1950. That means that 40% of the top leaders were already or nearly full grown adults before the model of immigration to Utah and the United States changed to a model of staying in the location where the person converted. Only five or 30% of the top fifteen were born after 1950, two in 1951, two in 1952, and one in 1955. Three of those five have only been in the top fifteen for under a year. Immigrating to America, more specifically Utah, to be Mormon used to be the expectation.

The quest for new stories is by nature two sided. A story needs to be both written and embraced to become a hero story. A story about a Mormon in Nigeria must capture the collective imagination to resonate with a readership beyond the borders of Nigeria, to grasp what is distinctivly Mormon and what is unique only to Nigeria. What stories will elucidate the dual passport experience common to all Mormons? A Mormon belongs to the vassal state as well as a legal nation state such as the Ukraine. Two identities merge or take priority at different times. Individuality already exists within the global Mormon vassal state, but the stories Mormons tell themselves need to reflect it. Already new stories have bubbled up from the international audience. Which ones will resonate and catch hold?

Global ties and a dual passport life is not new to Mormons, it's always been there. Mormons just need to see this familiar Mormon image from a different angle, a new paradigm. What seems far away or dissonant in a new paradigm may actually be very close and personal. Mormons used a dual identity or dual passports since the beginning. Men on Mormon missions without money and housing used competing identities for survival. A man might be British one minute when negotiating a bed for the night in India and Mormon the next day when differentiating himself from other preachers. A man might use his American identity to acquire a ship's passage home from Hong Kong to San Francisco then Mormon when he introduced himself on board to the Chinese he shared a deck with.

Would using a dual identity be similar to hyphenating like Jewish-American or African-American or Asian-American? Not exactly. Because Mormons can be chamelions, there is no way to identify them as Mormon, utilizing the identity in a given circumstance is up to individuals weighing out associated benefits or risk of harm. Because of correlation, though, diverse nationalities can communicate in a single language across the globe instantly if at least two sides choose to identify themselves in some way as Mormon. Diversity does not have to derive from crushing Mormon unifying efforts but playing on the essence of dueling identities within the vassal state.

Migration

How did a hearty vassal population of Britons, Europeans, some Polynesians and a few others, as well as pre-1850's Americans perceive diversity and inclusion in Utah? How might it have evolved over time isolated from mainstream America? Mormon leaders played with their own political chess pieces even as the US government monitored. Did federal officials, of whom some would've rather been anywhere but Mormon Utah, even notice the dashing stream of British and other multi-national immigration flowing into Great Salt Lake? Essentially Mormons operated by permission from the US government but with different perameters than the greater United States.

Britons today conceive of diversity and inclusion distinct and separately from Americans. Flying home from London after completing grad school in Reading, England in 2003, I sat next to a chatty South African about to rendezvous with his girlfriend in the United States. He rambled for longer than I would've hoped, weighing out the pros and cons of emigrating to the United States versus the United Kingdom. The logical choice, he said, would be to emigrate to the United States and finally settle down with his girlfriend, but then he fretted he would have to become American. In England, by contrast, he could still be South African with no expectation he take on English attitudes or behaviors. Britons might not fully integrate him into society but he could live side by side with them his own way. In the United States he feared losing his identity in the infamous American 'melting pot'.

He belabored the monologue convincing himself that his girlfriend was worth emigrating to the US. In the end, at least before he got off the plane, he intended to permanently settle in England rather than the US. Though, who knows what happened after explaining that to his girlfriend.

In the vassal state of Mormon Utah, they deal in an altered but heavily British population with British mindsets and customs. Some of whom, like my grandmother, remained in the same neighborhoods with the same friends they traveled with from Britain. Whole congregations, in fact, sometimes transplanted themselves together from northern England. It should be no surprise then that British culture heavily influenced Mormon conceptions of integration, diversity, and international relations compared with the average American outside of Utah.

Barring a coup, there is no expectation that a British ruler would be anyone but from a long line of British decent despite London's incredible international diversity. Racial tensions exhibit differently in England than in the US. People of color and even other Europeans become frustrated when they are always considered outsiders despite a multi-generational presence. For example, an Indian living in England may often be called an 'Indian' despite generations born and raised within England. Other minorities are grateful they are able to maintain their identities distinctive from British culture. They are not subjected to the 'melting pot' as we have mentioned. Each sovereign entity, or semi-sovereign as in the Mormon vassal state, runs on a social caste system. People at the top keep their power and influence by allowing a certain measure of inequality. Even though Britain and the US share many similar social dynamics, the variants are important when evaluating a highly dense British population isolated behind the Rocky Mountains.

Essentially the UK approached diversity and inclusion separately from the US. Britain controlled international sattelites through rule or partnerships with local leaders abroad before the 1850s. British-born Mormons took that model of international relations with them when they emigrated to Utah. Even today the Mormon vassal state's approach to international relations smells more British than American in that sense. Perhaps even Mormon appointed local leaders in international locations are far more versed, for better or worse, in the British model as well. They may conceive of diversity as differently from mainstream Americans in the US as the original Mormons in Utah differ from Americans.

Conceptions of the purposes and goals of diversity as well as its definition vary from region to region and person to person. Whether or not one particular approach to diversity is necessarily the correct way of viewing diversity is a separate question.

Distinctively Mormon

Section Two

Choose the Spouse

Leadership in the Mormon vassal state face other political and social variables different from the wider United States. For example, Mormon apostles in the top fifteen serve for life. Once a new apostle has been appointed, it is permanent. Rumors suggest that despite their unified face, behind the scenes certain personalities dominate consensus more often than ideal. Appointing, or in Mormon verbage, 'calling' men to fill top vacancies impacts the interpersonal dynamic among the fifteen on at least a weekly basis for years on end, more than anyone interacts in the vassal state as a whole. Living with someone's idiosyncrasies for the rest of their slowly aging life is a commitment on par with wedding vows.

Fifteen aging men who routinely advise programs, speak on new and stimulating topics, respect US law and social norms, and address the needs of populations of Mormons all across the globe, is more than rough, it's next to impossible. Recruiting men who might withstand these pressures is monumental. The First Presidency (the highest governing authority in the church consisting of three men) and the twelve apostles clock men for years before trusting them enough.

Americans including the international audience are now familiar with the United States' first elected African-American president, Barack Obama. Obama ushered in an era of affinity for diversity and inclusion across the globe. Conceptions about diversity are shifting all around the world to adjust to this revitalized American paradigm. Not for Mormons, though. Americans and Britons narrowed in to their select representatives to stereotype then grossly devalued any diversity or inclusion eminating from the global Mormon vassal state. Those American of American white bigots that inspire the songs of Broadway performers in Book of Mormon Musical are actually quite a small breed. You have to take a composite of the worst of several dual identity Mormons to find what they're singing. The composite might reverberate with some Mormons but it would be hard to find a whole community that actually looked or behaved that way. Then there are all African Mormons, especially in Uganda who not only really like being Mormon, but are often better Mormons than their compatriots in the United States. Book of Mormon Musical was written with a blindfold.

Yet it does seem like certain factions do dampen diversity and inclusion. Mormon leaders who didn't support and even fought the LGBTQi movement for equality and dignity reaches the top of the list of diverse averse behavior. Then not choosing a person of color to lead in the top fifteen also depressed some. One of the top leaders, President Russell M. Nelson thinks that millenials, or young people in their teens and twenties, should get on board with the church's stance but there is very little desire to hurt or offend friends and family members who are LGBTQi. The top may rule on certain issues but the bottom has to accept them for those points to eventually stick. My grandpa taught me that also. Just like a salacious point might be left out of the curriculum so also might a certain principle taught from the pulpit if the main body of Mormons does not accept it over time. Now that the global vassal state has grown so large outside of the United States, their acceptance or encouragement of policies also impacts these decisions.

But choosing a new leader who is a person of color would be exciting. Why couldn't this happen sooner? Barack Obama always had an eight year limit to his presidential run. Taking a gamble on diversity never carried the same stakes for Americans as appointing a diverse Mormon apostle whose term could run twenty to forty years. The commitment and impact would be much greater. Though internationalism and diversity have always been a part of Mormon Utah, it's only been about one generation since many of these towns have experienced racial variance and only since about the 1950s, two generations, when Mormons stopped asking converts to move to Utah.

Because Mormons are now located all over the globe, regional leaders increasingly originate from the regions in which they reside rather than transplanted from the center of the Mormon vassal state in the United States. Having two passports, one as a national of Paraguay plus a global Mormon vassal passport, accesses the center and all its satellites. Because Mormons are so actively involved in the social responsibilities of the vassal state, this engagement engenders potentially high exposure to multi-nationals within a global Mormon context.

But white American Utah has still dominated the culture to which other Mormons across the globe must bend, harkening back to the colonial battles of the mid-nineteenth century, right? Perhaps, though, other variables in play muddy the American colonial assertion. Which is it? Does an American or a largely British foundation and philosophy dominate the top fifteen leaders' approach to diversity within the Mormon sphere? Is it not British, in fact, to develop a proper way to speak and behave and then civilize the world with it? Is it even possible that needs from the vassal state's majority population outside of the US do not outweigh needs within the US? A larger population outside of the US on a practical logistical level naturally leads to slowly catering to global needs ahead of American needs. As time goes on, this shift will become more evident. Regimes across the world are sometimes more conservative, traditional and less open to human rights than Americans. Mormon inability to open to diversity might not be only a white cultural domination but a reverse colonialism emerging from countries where family is fundamental and LGBTQi are not accepted or even persecuted.

Colonialism, though, historically targeted trade, wealth and resources, using force as an alternative. Mormons volunteer. The backbone of the Mormon vassal state is socialism rather than capitalism, a compelling idea world-wide, which we will discuss later. Tithing and other religious donations, generally return to the communities from which they are collected. What economic advantage: trade, wealth or resources benefit Mormons by creating colonial empires abroad? Economic benefit in the vassal state's socialist organizational structure is shared and equal distribution is the norm. Mormons also adopted peaceful ideals in Mormon Utah, though at least one infamous massacre by rogue players mar that visage.

One colonial land grab still does irk. Until the 1950s Mormons asked converts to move to the Rocky Mountain area, which meant that Mormons' colonial land grab was Native-American land, now also known as the Mormon cooridor states of Utah, Idaho, Montana, Wyoming and Arizona. When Missouri and Illinois governors hustled off the Mormons from their purchased land, they turned Mormons into refugees. Refugees became colonists. Some Native-Americans still contest their presence especially for violent clashes where Native Americans were killed and sometimes even massacred. Recently the program that placed Native Americans in Mormon homes has come under fire as a colonialst enterprise. Some Mormon Native Americans, however, support the program which offered many a better life.

Colonialism implies forcing one culture upon another. All conversion to Mormonism is optional, though individuals have inappropriately coerced someone. The Mormon vassal state does not apologize for requiring converts to forsake other loyalties and adhere to certain values and social norms. Debateable though, is whether those values and norms are American, or even fully 1850s British, but actually a dynamic morphing of multi-nationals' high exposure to each other and unique Mormon constraints. Top leadership, mostly American-born, still define the course despite expanding diversity just as has been the case since the 1830s. Mormon interaction and participation with the wider world, including the United States, may drive Mormon leadership to become more mainstream American.

Perhaps the mix of Euro-British and American Mormons that emigrated to Utah from generations of povery and meager education need a few generations to understand themselves and the world. Many were shut out of economic and political strategic decision making because of their low status for centuries. Adjusting expectations for the relatively new wealthy and educated, may promote positive connections with generational Mormons in Utah and clearer logic for top leadership appointments. Mormons like Mitt Romney, the Marriotts and other entreprenuers and business owners have gained lots of wealth but its relatively recent wealth. Communicating effectively who Mormons are socially as well as religiously may assist the Mormon vassal state's global diplomacy efforts. Vibrant debates about social issues are the mark of a maturing society.

Since the 1950s, local populations in the Mormon vassal state's sattelites across the globe emerged, as 'stakes' or networks of Mormons bound together by location. Local, native representation increasingly becomes the new pattern. In this state of flux, choosing new top Mormon leaders who are people of color to lead from the vassal state's captial of Salt Lake City is an interesting proposition given Mormon's unique and isolated history.

The global audience, Mormon and non-Mormon alike, might find it useful to assess Mormons in Utah as distinct cultural actors, not necessarily as the Americans they see or read about in the news. Mormon satellites, or vassals hosted by governments outside the US, might need the same time to develop their own multi-generational presence outside of Utah distinctive from their own cultures.

I Don't Own a Kettle

Conditions within Mormonism itself applied over a century engendered a shared culture distinct from American, British or European influences; one that is developing among global Mormon sattelites after only one or two generations. One distinctly Mormon vassal state characteristic morphed away from its Euro-American influence evolved over coffee. Let me illustrate with three stories of how the absence of coffee in a society forms an identity apart from an individual refraining from coffee for health reasons.

Coffee at Brigham Young University.

Once on a Saturday morning I crossed an almost diserted BYU campus. A woman shuffled up to me, relieved, and said, "Thank God." Immediately I knew she was a foreigner (not how most Mormons use the phrase in Provo). She said, I'm here for a conference and I'm desperate for a cup of coffee.

I'm cutting an inward smile oozing out my ears despite my attempt at serious concern. I'm sorry. BYU doesn't sell coffee. You won't be able to buy it on campus, I said.

She seemed a little annoyed, Ok then, how about a Coke or a Dr. Pepper?

Sorry, I said, you can't buy caffeinated drinks either. The BYU Bookstore has a bar selling chocolates, though.

Even more irritated she said, Well then off campus, where can I get a coffee? Just get me to a cup of coffee.

I couldn't help her. I finally said, I'm Mormon. We're Mormon. We don't drink coffee. There's probably a place to buy coffee around here but I have no idea where. Sorry.

With a roll of her eyes, she huffed away. And I should also be completely annoyed when they didn't sell me a taco in Tel Aviv. And what's wrong with the Taiwanese who only served me dried reconstituted cheese they felt impelled to emphasize was actually mold? And for the life of me, why does it cost so darn much to buy a wee bottle of peanut butter in London?

Next story.

One of my Provo High students decided to host an Iraqi school principal. She flew in from Iraq and upon meeting my student's in-house dog quickly called begging me to stay at my place instead. Hence I quite unexpectedly hosted an Iraqi woman in my apartment.

Within minutes of setting down her luggage she requested a cup of coffee.

I don't have any coffee.

What, you ran out?

No. I don't drink coffee.

Why not?

Remember coffee is an important part of the Arab culture of hospitality with perhaps even more significance than the US coffee culture although if it isn't clear yet, I'm not one to talk. I know as much about Arab coffee culture as American.

I explained to her that I'm Mormon, etc etc. She said, a bit exasperated, Well, you'll certainly let me drink coffee, won't you.

Of course, I said, blinking without the slightest idea of what to do about it next.

Well then let's go to the store, she said, but I gulped.

Glancing around for Provo High students and ecclesiastical leaders or for anyone I might have to explain to later, I determined that no one would see me. Worse, I didn't want people to hypothesize about what I was doing. Coffee is a signal not just of rebellion but could also indicate that a person doesn't value the culture in which they grew up. It took me a while to even find the coffee aisle.

But then I spied it. I'd assumed there'd be a tin next to the Ovaltine labeled 'coffee'. I had no idea there were different *kinds* of coffee, shelf after shelf in fact. I turned to her, Alright, here's the coffee. You can choose which one you'd like.

But the fun didn't end there. I'm accustomed to *NesCafe* in Iraq. While I'm in America, I want to try other kinds of American coffee. Why don't you suggest one.

Gulp again.

The shelves of coffee blurred together. On second thought I told her, I really think you should pick the coffee. I don't drink coffee so I wouldn't know which kind is best.

She kept insisting, But certainly you've heard of a good brand. No doubt her views of American inhospitality compared to the much warmer Middle East rolled across her mind.

Looking again I decided that since I like mint-flavored hot chocolate I would suggest the mint-flavored coffee.

Relieved and back at my apartment she asked for a kettle to boil the water. I hadn't thought of that either. I didn't have one. Didn't even own a mug.

She drank her first mint-flavored coffee from a glass with water heated in the microwave. Apparently, as I quickly learned, mint-flavored coffee is disgusting.

You really don't know anything about coffee, do you? she said. Hopefully she realized that this wasn't the America she had visited on the east coast and not offering coffee wasn't a sign of inhospitality.

No. Sorry.

I borrowed a kettle and a mug from grandma the next day. Mormon really is its own dimension.

Last story.

I was taking lunch during an all-day assignment interpreting for a seminar. I had moved only a few weeks previously to DC from Utah. A guy from the seminar came up to me smiling and said, Would you like to get coffee with me later?

Somewhere in the back of my head I knew this didn't necessarily mean he actually expected me to drink coffee. I'd never actually been in a coffee shop before. In my mind I started flashing through all the movies I'd seen where guys ask girls for coffee, like some sort of business meeting. I finally realized that I was taking too long to respond and ended up saying the only thing that came to mind, I don't drink coffee.

Ok, how 'bout dinner, then? he said, a bit more determined. Oh. I realized. It's a date.

Later my co-interpreter accused me of flirting with a client. No really, I said, I was caught a bit off guard. I didn't realize what he meant by 'getting coffee' right away.

Sure you didn't, she said, Everyone knows what coffee means. I'm still not an expert on coffee culture. But, apparently everyone knows what coffee means. Americans know what coffee means. Mormons who are not bi-cultural might not, yet. Mormons differ from typical mainstream Americans.

Pyramids

As a vassal state which developed independently from the rest of the United States and then spread abroad linking people from all over the world, Mormonism also has developed its own approach to diversity quite different from what formulated among American liberals in other parts of the US.

American liberals often acuse Mormons of having no savvy on issues of diversity. By adjusting our paradigms we might see that the Mormon paradigm of diversity is equally as robust as the American Liberal approach, just very different and not necessarily just because of its strong British-Euro component.

The Western liberal, and particularly in the US, approaches diversity built from at least one core premise. Equality is vital, measured by the ability to rise economically, politically, or in any other way an individual deems necessary to succeed. Imagine a pyramid with the poor at the bottom and wealthy educated elites at its point. American liberalism seeks for all people no matter their station, race, religion, place of origin,

98

sexuality, etc to have the opportunity to rise within the pyramid. Some of the rhetoric that attends this Equality of the Rise are phrases like, 'American Dream,' meaning the possibility to become wealthy no matter how poor you started. The 'glass ceiling,' meaning a person who was not permitted to rise beyond a certain point. 'I want my children to look at their leaders and see people that look like them,' often meaning they would like to believe that someone from their station or racial origin could someday rise to that height to create opportunity for their segment of diversity.

The rhetoric focuses on the rise. An entire Western culture of humanitarianism developed around the ability to rise. People group themselves together to elevate their own representatives in the competition for economic or political rise. Those who succeed in rising first are celebrated. 'The first African American to achieve…', 'The first woman to achieve….', etc.

Western liberals realized in the quest to rise, silos developed and groups weren't sharing best practices or resources to elevate others. Activism focused on women and girls may not include women of African descent or women with disabilities. Activism aimed for Black men might not consider Transgender experiences. They realized the silos didn't always fit certain unique individuals. For example, what happens when a person is African-American, Female, *and* a Person with a Disability?

So a new concept evolved called Intersectionality. It means that within one person several different identities intersect. Which one silo, for example, should that individual preference in their desire for equality (of the rise)? With multiple identities a new dynamic surfaced that didn't belong to any of the original silos. For example, if you eat a torilla and cheese separately they each taste a certain way. If you shred the cheese and sprinkle it over the taco then grill it nice and crispy, you have the same two incredients but a taste unique. It's a quesadilla.

The concept of privilege also developed. American liberals realized that some groups had an easier time rising and staying elevated than others. Groups who rose more quickly or easily held a certain privilege that others didn't have. To recognize when a person holds a privilege over another in the efforts to rise is considered intelligent. But it's more complicated than that. Because people have multiple identities there might be some situations when they exercise privilege and other times when they don't. Admitting that additional layer of complexity designates a person who is compoundly enlightened.

Let's take the example of a white woman from Spain. As a Spaniard she may experience privilege over Spanish speakers in other countries but might be at a disadvantage in the English speaking UK. As a white person she might have privilege over people of color but as a woman she might have less privilege than a man.

Let's try another one. What about an Asian-American, homosexual man? As an American he has a certain privilege over others. As a man he may have privilege over women in many cases but as a homosexual he might be at a disadvantage. As an Asian-American he may also have a disadvantage in some spheres and the advantage in others depending on the situation. Intersectionality would mean that when combining his characteristics, a new unexpected dynamic arises. Boiled down, this American Liberal discussion is largely based on the premise of equality in the ability to rise.

Mormon diversity is also very robust but focuses on a different, counter approach to diversity, inclusion, and equality. Mormons focus instead on the Equality of the Fall. Originally Mormons were mainly working class or lower middle-class tradesmen and farmers from New England and Europe trying to adjust to an industrializing society where the ability to rise was locked, chaining them forever to their impoverished life styles. Only a very select few could rise. These farmers and tradesmen were socialistic in nature, economically and organizationally, in the early days of Mormon growth. Bringing down the haughtiness of the rich and elite made more sense than forging a path to the top, a value that brought everyone down to an equal plane ensuring another type of equality. Equality at the bottom.

Thus we get a working class value of Equality of the Fall. The Equality of the Rise really comes from a top down perspective. Look at how much I have, I want to share it with others. Working class socialists may seek quality of life but there has always been, in working class populations around the world, disdain for elitist position, the power of money to corrupt, and inaccessible education. Once someone rises, that new wealth doesn't seem to trickle to the base as well as hoped and definitely not fairly. Not everyone can become elite with titles and education but everyone can be poor and the working class know that well.

Equality at the bottom is much more attainable. Mormons might frame it as inspiration revealed from a Higher Power. Deity, for example, understanding that most of the world's population are poor, inspired farmers and tradesmen in a way to approach 'fairness' before imparting that divine knowledge to an educated elite. In other words diety might talk to the people of which poverty affects. Or in a secular sense, people in poverty might have the best knowledge bank for pulling themselves out of it. Whether you believe it was their social situation that inspired them or deity is a personal matter. For now, we'll focus on the social dynamics of the value of the fall.

Mormons no longer employ economic socialism in their professional lives but it still exists in church organization and function. Not to mention that all Mormon assignments are unpaid and volunteer including at the very top (though with full time callings some are given stipends on which to subsist if needed). The fall in this sense means that nearly anyone, no matter how high their position could fall. There is enough room for that type of equality because the pyramid is much wider at the bottom. Nearly everyone can experience the bottom of the pyramid at some point though not everyone will experience elitism at its apex no matter the activism. Mormon rhetoric reflects the value of taking a turn at the bottom and even glorifies it to some extent.

Phrases like, 'All callings are equally important,' meaning even the lowest assignment you receive from church leaders is important. 'I might be bishop today but I'll be working in the Nursery tomorrow.' (I've heard this phrase from several Mormon leaders.) This means that although they have a respected position at the moment, even they could be given what many Mormons consider to be one of the most trying assignments, which is taking care of toddlers for two hours every week while everyone else attends class. Another phrase, 'Don't aspire to callings,' meaning Mormons don't value an attitude of rising above others. Bishops, for example, are expected to role up their sleeves and get to work along side everyone else.

Mormons, like Muslims and others, fast once a month to remember the poor, donate, and practice humility. All Mormons whether they like their neighborhood or not attend a church meeting within a ward (or boundary), which originally referred to the ward of a city and still references that general meaning. The boundaries of these wards, though, are drawn by Mormon leaders for Mormon purposes and don't correlate to actual city wards any longer.

The Mormon approach to inclusion and diversity results in the same types of challenges other socialist organizations encounter. Specialization and standing out are discouraged. For example, the church's office building for administrators is filled with underpaid and overworked staff. The rhetoric is that these workers would rather work for free but we pay them just enough to support their families. It shouldn't be a surprise that it isn't always easy to attract the most talented who'd rather get paid according to their work ethic and talent on the market, though there are exceptions and some are quite talented.

The pyramid's baseline for women is nearly impossible to nail down. Motherhood became the lowest common denominator but because that goal as a baseline isn't practical or feasible, Mormon women have been speaking out against that measure of equality. Men are encouraged to succeed professionally but only with at least a nod to caring for others, meaning that men earn money out of necessity and not principally for gain. But no Mormon man I know courts a girl bragging about all the ditches he's dug in his life, either.

Fluent

What does the Equality of the Fall look like in relation to the rest of the United States? Mitt Romney's 2008 and 2012 campaigns for US president highlights the opposing values of the Mormon vassal state and the host United States.

Mitt Romney grew up in a bicultural, bilingual environment compared to Mormons growing up in a majority Mormon culture in Utah. He seemed to speak American fluently, though some may debate that. However, Americans who know little about the Mormon vassal state wanted to know more before they elected him. The problem became how to adequately convey his Mormon story. The public came to know pieces of the story but wanted the behind the scenes version, and understandably.

Romney on the public stage lifted the lid of the box a peak only to arouse more curiousity. At the same time detractors turned his Mormonness into a joke. People thought he was trying to come off too humble and wanted him to present his Mormon background more forthrightly. More than humbleness might have fed the dynamic or to some, the apparent cover up. Romney juggled opposing values of diversity and inclusion, the Equality of the Rise versus Mormon's Equality of the Fall.

Every time Romney promoted himself for his campaign he favored an American identity. But Mormon values pit him against self-promotion. The tension between the two may be familiar to some Mormons with dual citizenship, Mormon and American or Mormon and Mexican or Mormon and Russian, in secular contexts. Perhaps more than personality and values were at stake. To promote Mormon accomplishments and service too much might be an internal conflict for Romney. He might even risk votes from Mormons who wouldn't mind him promoting business success but who would shrink from his promotion of success, though Mormons would label it as 'service', within the Mormon vassal state. Beyond the vote, he might endanger his Mormon social networks that last beyond a presidential run.

Mitt Romney's noticeable tension between his professional and personal religious life must consider too many confounding variables to conclusively isolate personality, political expediency and Mormon values. Perhaps the tension itself occurs for other Mormons reconciling the Mormon vassal state's culture and values with their host nation's in a secular arena.

Let's travel to the Mormon vassal state's peripheries, to Washington DC for other evidences of the dynamic. CNN's Religion editor, Dan Gilgoff, wrote in 2012 that DC was suprisingly a Mormon stronghold. Mormons congregate in the social units of wards comprising anyone, rich, poor, ethnic, or racial group, who lives within those boundaries and are responsible to care for each other. They meet weekly for a church service and religious instruction but strong social ties reach beyond that meeting into the week.

In Washington DC, ward boundaries draw together diverse people and circumstances. Among Mormons you will see a swanky downtown lawyer teaching a doctrinal class for a year or two. In his next assignment he's keying a popping tune on a piano for the children's group. An Afghani limosine driver will speak his truth from the pulpit to State Department diplomats sitting in the congregation. A Democrat in the Senate will listen to the single thirty-something software company employee. One minute a bishop leads the congregation. The next he's tying Cub Scout knots. Everyone gets an assignment (calling). And further, everyone expects they will receive an assignment at the bottom at one time or another.

Equality of the Fall. In other words, there's room enough for all at the bottom regardless of a person's unique circumstances or background. No silos. No need for marches. Start promoting yourself among Mormons, though, and the room could get chilly.

Japanese Mormon men who led their congregation and then were released to serve in 'lesser' assignments (relative to the society outside of the Mormon vassal state) struggle with the accompanying disgrace or loss of face the 'demotion' causes. Coupled with the Mormon ban on alcohol, their standing within the wider non-Mormon Japanese community suffers compoundly. Some create their own businesses to sustain themselves and their families independent of the Japanese non-Mormon community.

Does this phenomenon occur in Japan because Mormonism is an American institution imposing American values upon the Japanese or because Mormonism is Mormon, rooted in influences unique to itself despite its subordination to US law and norms? The expectation of an eventual demotion is not particularly American nor is the prohibition on alcohol American protocol since a century ago. Japanese face a conflict between Japanese and Mormon cultures, the Mormon part of which is not or no longer mainstream American.

Americans meeting a Japanese man would welcome him with, Can I get you a cup of coffee or tea? When his work promotes him, Americans throw a cocktail party.

Imagine this scenario translated linearly into Mormon. The Mormon points to the mug and says, What's that you're drinking? ...Yeah?

Grabbing the mug as the liquid swishes its sides, Well, you won't be needing that anymore.

Then instead of a promotion a new position might go something like this, and I'm not kidding, You inspired people with your ability to manage that program. How do you feel about vacuuming floors? We'd now like you to clean the building every week for a month.

Don't worry, in real life, Mormons would let him finish the cup of tea first. I'm a little joking, but only a little.

Will you find Mormons in the vassal state who violate its social code? Of course. Individuals, despite the values, continue moving up the leadership ladder instead of receiving a demotion. Financial security and upward mobility in their professional lives and stable family lives are tanamount to Mormon properness (righteousness). In many Mormon minds, the reason a person succeeds in the outside economy is not because he or she sought it but because it was rewarded for good behavior, another socialist ideal. Mormons, though, actually might oogle over someone in a 'higher' position or aspire to more visible assignments. Sometimes people don't receive an assignment (calling), tantamount to a mild to moderate form of ocstericism done purposefully or not. Mormons name drop and promote agendas. The social ideals of Mormonism are like the vacation home. In day to day living you will spot dirt in the corners.

There is an element of rise that has existed since the beginning among Mormons. Anyone could become a leader no matter what race, ethnicity, national origin, or how uneducated or menial their job, and slowly even including sexual orientation. A construction worker might lead the congregation, etc. This is common.

You actually have to break the code or bend it to discriminate and people do. For example, perhaps I'm supposed to have an assignment but my Mormon leader doesn't agree with my decisions, or my politics, my race, or doesn't like that I'm a woman, etc. Mormon code requires him to assign me a calling but he may leave me in the Nursery for years on end or claim he's too busy after a full year of waiting to assign me a calling at all. It might be hard to contend

111

discrimination because serving at the bottom is expected, though not forever. Luckily leaders on the local and regional level are rotated out to balance for these types of problems. Women have been shut out from decisions that affect them. It's not a perfect system but the socialist equality at the bottom conception is compelling.

People of color need to occupy leadership roles all the way up to the highest levels because their affinities will vary, valuing people of color that others might not fully notice. Requesting more people of color at the 'highest' levels of Mormon leadership is antithetical to the Mormon psyche of not seeking for position unfortunately.

The discourgement of people of color seeking a position among the top fifteen is not just white discrimination. It's not just that the Mormon base in Utah has been predominantly white and needs to learn about others' culture. It is also against the very unique values of the Mormon vassal state; antithetical for Mormons to seek after lofty position and self promotion. It's also competing with a conception of diversity which evolved independently from the rest of the United States. Equality and inclusion happen at the bottom of the pyramid, not the top. At the top there are not enough positions to spread around, establishing true equality.

Does this phenomenon occur because Mormonism is American? It is because Mormonism is Mormon rooted in influences both American, British, international, and dynamically changing with large influxes of converts across the globe?

Kumbaya

American liberal conceptions of diversity
mythologize the kumbaya moment when everyone
comes together in a measure of peace and harmony
despite their differences. Peace and harmony only
allow for a certain range of acceptance, not
complete acceptance of everyone and every idea.
Certain people and ideas are in direct conflict with
each other. Imagine a needle that when placed
becomes the epicenter of what is acceptable
behavior and belief. Spiralling away from that
needle acceptance wanes.

American liberal conceptions of diversity
and inclusion hover the needle with the loudest
voice for equality and then the range extends from
that point. When African-Americans campaign for
rights and inclusion, the needle hovers near their
movement and those who support it, ranging
outward. When LGBTQi crusade for rights,
respect, and marriage equality, the needle hovers
around those who support their movement ranging
outward. The needle swings depending on who is
most dominant and on disciplined message. The
loudest voice is usually the most well-funded and
organized.

The LGBTQi movement is brilliant, well-funded, well-organized, needed, but also siloed. Activist leaders may or may not choose to expend resources to promote other causes such as an African-American, Black Lives Matter, movement. It would be in their best interest to choose causes that would also maximize their own goals. If the cause to create equality for people with disabilities, which is also siloed, does not have the funding and no other cause will mutually benefit from their rise, their cause will struggle. Thus, LGBTQi's marriage equality is upheld in the US Supreme Court but the United Nations Treaty on the Rights of Persons with Disabilities fails to ratify in the US Congress. A liberal's credentials are not based on their support of the rights of persons with disability solely but hinges on their support for LGBTQi and African-Americans. When certain Mormon ideas fall outside of the range created by this needle, Mormons are no longer included or considered 'diverse'. Mormon support for Syrian refugees' resettlement in Utah does not overcome their lack of full support for LGBTQi.

The Mormon needle for diversity and inclusion falls on a minimal baseline set of beliefs subject to 'modern revelation' which, for our purposes, allows for some movement in the needle. This means that although a 'revelation' may come from diety one day, the next day another 'revelation' may completely discard or significantly alter the previous one.

The needle is also set on a local level by each individual ward. If the ward boundaries include people who all think the same, you'll think Mormons aren't very diverse. However, if the ward boundaries include diverse thinking styles, cultures, ages, races, political persuasons, you'll think Mormons tolerate a great deal of diversity. There is not much difference between the range of acceptance within the Mormon community and the range of acceptance within the Western liberal community except that the centers of gravity for the range of people who are accepted are set differently.

People at Mormon church are often offended. Offending people and how to avoid or overcome it often comes up in Mormon discourse. There's an attitude that people become offended over minor ditties then leave the church in a huff. This attitude of not tolerating difference of opinion, of course, angers people with real concerns and frustrations. The fact that people do become offended, however, is a healthy sign that Mormons are diverse enough to cause offence. People can find corners and pockets of Mormons for acceptance of a wide array of ideas but maybe not in a farm town inculcated with descendents from one polygamous family. Mormons must

116

move out of a ward boundary to avoid people they don't feel comfortable among. Moving out of a ward as a last resort to dodge people and ideas is a strong sign liberals and conservatives and a host of other ideas were coexisting enough to make someone want to leave to find people more like themselves. In a world where people can avoid an opposing point of view by flipping the channel, Mormon diversity is quite exceptional.

Yet Mormons are still overwhelmingly white in the center, in Utah and especially in the top fifteen leaders. The Western liberal approach to diversity has much merit. When a person of color is in a position of leadership, he or she makes unusual decisions, views people differently, affiliates with new institutions, and builds new affinities. Might American leaders in the top fifteen prophet and apostles, though, be necessary for the vassal state's continued legal relations with the US government? Are allowing global sattelites and people of color to preserve their own communities and cultures preferable to leading intercultural and international dynamics on an international scale from Salt Lake? Competing conceptions of diversity and its role are in play.

Conservative?

Zoom in for a moment to Provo about forty-five minutes by car south of the modern capital of Salt Lake City and twenty minutes north of my grandma's hometown of Springville. Home to Brigham Young University, Provo neighbors another college town of Orem home to Utah Valley University. More than Salt Lake City, Mormons densely populate Provo and Orem. A lot of Mormons who attend BYU and UVU are unaware of the unique dynamics of the more settled non-student parts of town, which we will highlight. Provo is also home to one of the largest Fourth of July Freedom Festival celebrations in the country. People there are proud to be American. How do we dare propose Provo as a global city within the Mormon vassal state?

Developed quite independently from the US and thriving on Mormonism's unique characteristics, all the Fourth of July fireworks in the world don't necessarily make it particularly American except perhaps the influences borrowed from television, radio and country music of mainstream US elsewhere.

A friend of mine from Provo grew up loving country music, for example. She was in her twenties before she realized that all the songs she loved were about a foreign land (Tennessee and the South) among people she'd only met when they visited Utah.

What determines 'Americanness' in the vassal state distinct from Mormoness? This question is similar for countries who adopt other cultures or phrases. When Japanese say the word, 'pinku' are they using the English word 'pink' or is it now culturally appropriated and should be considered Japanese? Is listening to Tennessee's music still Southern or now culturally appropriated Mormon music?

Drive down to Provo High School, just across the street from Brigham Young University's southern rim, though the school will soon move to west Provo. From the outside it has looked like many other high schools in the United States, brown brick with a large green bulldog mascot sign, a track out back surrounding a football field with bleachers. There's a driver's range, a separate science building, an auditorium, a main office, music rooms, and several academic wings. One unique building high schools outside of Utah wouldn't necessarily have is a Mormon Seminary. There are so many Mormons attending Provo High

School that on site religious education is offered to students as an elective.

These high school students fall into the same types of groups as other schools in less Mormon environments. They deal with many of the same sorts of problems and temptations as most other teens, despite what some Mormons outside of Utah fantacize, i.e. a Provo immune to vices and temptations. They watch many of the same television shows and movies. It's easy to believe they are just like any other Americans with a few cultural variations one might expect of any region of the United States.

Utah is also famous for its political conservatism. The last time I was in Provo, 'liberal' was almost a bad word. Though, they might not be as conservative as they think. Barack Obama's win over Mormon Mitt Romney in the 2012 US presidential election awakened the possibility of mislabeling of Mormon values and culture. A society full of historically recent immigrants, newly educated decendents of tradesmen and farmers who adopt others' cultures and values shouldn't be suprised reality doesn't match what they supposed. For example, if Southerners love America and Mormons love America then Southerners might become a model to predominantly Euro-Mormons for how to love America.

Turns out Mitt Romney, who holds some of the standard views of many Mormons in the United States, wasn't 'conservative enough' for many Republicans in his political party. The views for which he was 'conservative enough', did not line up with some Mormons including the top fifteen leaders, whose policies often don't fit well on the American political spectrum. Mormons don't fit well because they evolved independently from most of the US. Mormons that do fit the spectrum may actually be Americans.

Moving Forward

Section Three

Car Magazine

Back to Provo High. I had the good fortune of both attending Provo High as a student for four years then later teaching there for five more years. Dynamics in the interim had changed dramatically. While I taught at Provo High one of the assistant principals explained the administration's struggle recruiting more teens of color into the Provo High student government, which at the time was still all white.

Here's roughly how she explained the dilemma. The student body had been about 90-95% white. Fast foward a few years later and the ratios had dramatically altered to more like 60/40% white to non-white students. The majority of the new non-Mormon population were Latino students, though some white students were not Mormon and some Latino students were Mormon. Recently re-drawn borders clumped the city's growing Latino neighborhoods with Provo High where it had once been equally spread between both high schools in town. From the ground it looked and smelled like racism. The richer sister school may have actually created a disadvantage for themselves, however. Because of the sudden almost equal ratios of white students (including non-Mormons) to Latinos and other students of color, Provo High students would learn cultural plurality by necessity, leaving the whiter sister school behind.

Despite the administration's efforts, they and the current student government officers couldn't seem to lure Latino students to run for office. When they succeeded, the white population easily out-voted them to support their own peer favorites. Re-evaluating, the administration realized that traditional school events didn't cater to Latino students' interests or their logistical and practical needs. For example, Latino students often worked after school to support their families. Latino students seemed to prefer their own socials and their own popularity competitions rather than the popularity of student government. They hadn't resolved the quandary before I moved to Washington, DC.

Administrators furrowed their eyebrows stretching for ways to integrate the substantial influx of Latino students. Cultural plurality became urgent to curb the rise of gang and other types of violence and misbehavior. None of their white students' parents, who had attended when the school was nearly all white, could offer much advice let alone modeling to their sons and daughters. When I studied at Provo High, it was as the assistant principal said, almost all white. I can vouch for this relatively overnight dramatic change having been a student at Provo High School only twelve years earlier.

Cities the size of Provo/Orem with university towns in the United States have dealt with diversity for many more years. Logically Provo/Orem must have a serious racial problem if the white population is so high. Other comparable cities to Provo/Orem with all white populations do have a history of racial laws specifically to keep people of color out. Perhaps a state or city law had discouraged African Americans or other people of color from moving to Utah.

Because of this predominantly white dynamic, people steer away from Utah Mormons assuming racism lies at the heart of the reason for the few people of color in Utah. Perhaps it does. We saw it, for example, in the boundary divisions between the two high schools in Provo. Racism is definitely easy to believe. After all, if a group is all white, they are probably racist, there may be no other reasons for the white dominance. If a high school's student government is all white, then there must be racism however subtle or covert. Turns out there are many evidences that Utah Mormons have said and done racist things some overtly, some subtly, some naively. There are quite a few scholars and bloggers and even a Broadway musical to point out racist words and actions though they tend to point to African-American racism rather than racism toward Latinos.

If you ask Utahns about racism, many will deny it. Some will say, but I don't even know any African-Americans let alone very many other people of color (besides Latinos, that is). Sometimes the first time they've met a person of color is on their Mormon two-year proselyting mission. Amidst widespread accusations of racism sometimes Mormons within Utah feel belittled rather than educated about it. It's also harder to grasp a more subtle form of racism called 'systematic racism' where just because a person hasn't met a person of color doesn't mean the system doesn't promote white people at the expense of people of color.

Systematic racism in short is the idea that the overall system itself is racist and keeps people of color from moving into places like Utah, for example. If they do move in it prevents them from moving up the social hierarchy. Three new Mormon apostles (top fifteen leaders) named in 2015 are white and American citizens, symbolizing for many that Mormon leadership simply does not care about diversity. They're racist and don't understand the dynamics of the international body of Mormon members. People can also point to the Mormon ban on people of

African descent holding the priesthood lifted in 1978. The ban even extended to people beyond the borders of the United States. This is unexcuseable racism no matter how inocent or naive.

Although the Latino population in Utah grows exponentially, Mormon scholars primarily focus on racial dynamics between white Utah Mormons and African-Americans, Africans, or others of African descent. This leaves wide gaps in the study of the Mormon vassal state as a whole. How do other sattelite vassal cultures discriminate, for example? Are white Utah Mormons the only Mormons who discriminate and is racism the only method of discrimination? Sometimes these scholars study a specific subsection of the global Mormon vassal state but label them with the all inclusive label of 'Mormons' rather than distinguishing to which segment they are referring. Their analysis does not refer to 'Mormons' but Mormons in Utah and not even all Mormons in Utah. Who, I wonder, are they specifically talking about? American-born Mormon generational converts? British-born Mormon generational converts, who might need an additional analysis of British history and politics to explain dynamics? German-born?

When African Americans began leaving the South in droves, not many moved to Utah. When I casually asked an African American historian in Virginia about this, the answer I received went something like, Mormons just don't want people of diversity to move there. He listed laws discouraging African Americans from moving to other states but when it came to Utah, he didn't know of a specific law discouraging people of color. But he leaned in with a wink and was sure something must be going on out there among those Mormons. Good thing he didn't know I was one of those Mormons from Utah. Had he stigmatized Mormons or assumed I didn't look or act like a stereotypical Mormon? He knew other states were racist and even enacted laws to discourage African Americans from moving in but Utah was a bit of a mystery.

It turns out there was a law in 1852 that discouraged African Americans from moving to Utah. Congress pressured Utah Territory to keep the delicate balance between free and slave states. For Utah's economic survival, becoming a federalized state of the Union was vital. The Utah legislature enacted a law stating that any enslaved persons would still retain that status within Utah. After the Emancipation Proclamation of January 1, 1863, this Utah law became null and void. The cause to fit into the greater US mainstream, though, continued to engender white ideals at the expense of people of color.

Scolars of race remind us that Brigham Young held racist views and enacted racist policies. Young wasn't a pillar of support for diversity. Women also suffered under his gaze. Joseph Smith's widow didn't even get along with him. Young was born in Vermont forming many of his ideas, like most adults, about race and women by twenty-nine years old before he first read the Book of Mormon and became Mormon at thirty-one. It is important to note that Joseph Smith was quite progressive for his time toward racial diversity and women, though.

Brigham Young's strengths lied in mass migration and government building, leading Mormons from the US and Europe into the west and then forming an expansive economic and political network. With droughts and starving refugees crowding into Great Salt Lake, people he believed who demanded attention or special consideration were not tolerated well. Some Mormons still bristle at a few of Young's influential policy decisions that reverberate even today.

The federal government did finally grant Utah statehood in 1896. The 1852 law forcing people to remain enslaved while in Utah became nullified after the Civil War. A religious ban on priesthood authority wouldn't have prevented African Americans from moving to Utah necessarily, but might have discouraged them from becoming Mormons. No law forced African Americans or anyone to become Mormon while in Utah. Governing institutions slowly reverted to secular elected officers like other states and territories within the Union. In 1857 when President Buchanan ordered US troops to Utah to ensure a new territorial governor Brigham Young left his guvenatorial post. African Americans might have moved to Utah just like any other state but still remained outside the Mormon vassal state.

Let's imagine that Mormons were just as racist as their neighbors, strongly discouraging African-Americans to move to Utah. Could it also be possible that African Americans, often deeply religious, and even other people of color felt wary of moving to Mormon country where rumors of polygamy and strange religious practices originated? Might they have thought they would be forced to convert? Even after other parts of the United States who had also passed discriminatory laws became more diverse, African Americans still shied away from Utah as did other people of color. The diversity that now permeates Utah in growing numbers appears to come from groups with little prior knowledge of popular fables of the strange stereotyped 'American' Mormons.

After the Civil War Utah's discriminatory law against African-Americans was null and void but still no large influxes moved in except for in trickles or with the railroad. With very few people of color in Utah except Native-Americans, some Polynesians, and especially few African-Americans, racism within social hierarchy would not be a particularly effective underclass in an almost all white society. If there are very few people of color, who do elites, Mormons or otherwise, step on to solidify their wealth and prestige?

Racism as a social caste system is barely feasible in an almost all white society until the last decade. All societies, though, have social hierarchies of some sort where the elites have a stake in keeping a designated underclass at bay. The social caste system in Utah wouldn't be effective along racial lines until there were enough people of other races to make that hierarchy feasible. This does not mean there wasn't a dogged dedication to whiteness or systematic racism in policy or relations toward the outside world. What this means is that racism as an internal social hierarchy within a white population hardly not feasible. Other discriminatory designations promote others above their neighbors. Racism without many of other races is ambiguous among a white population and Utahns reflect that ambiguousness when asked about it.

Some people at this point would say that I don't get racism. But I do believe many Mormons in Utah are racist. Even if there were few or even no people of color in Utah, Mormons have made racist comments about interracial marriage, and a host of other hot topics. Mormons still struggle with racism. I'll define how, then share a story.

Racism in Utah is learned belief and behavior in three ways: 1) people brought their experiences with and beliefs about race with them when they become Mormons; 2) through outside pressures and influences whether it be laws, political expediency, or media; or 3) fear of the new and different. The Mormon vassal state in the larger American federal and economic system, adjusts to the ebbs and flows of US government laws and social trends to survive.

If Mormons are racist whether directly or indirectly, this is a serious problem. As long as racism is learned behavior and not the actual social hierarchy that traditionally cemented the elites' position in Utah, racism should also be more often than not, be unlearned.

Let me take you into one of my beginning American Sign Language classes at Provo High. Most of my students were white with a few Latinos (most Latinos took Spanish or French as their language elective). Two white boys started harassing one of the Latino boys using racially charged comments so I decided to address the problem on a broader scale with the entire class.

A few class periods later, I asked everyone to anonymously write down any questions or concerns about racism and specifically the dynamics between Latino and white students. I gathered up their papers, shuffled them so I couldn't guess who had written which comments, and then read them aloud to the students.

Over and over students commented about how they didn't know what to do or how to interact with Latino students. They didn't understand the language and they thought people might be talking about them. Some had tried to invite Latino class mates to events or parties but they didn't show up or didn't respond. Some girls felt insecure when Latino boys catcalled them in the halls. Some had asked their parents for suggestions but their parents didn't offer workable solutions. They expressed desire to learn how to improve their relationship with Latinos at school.

After reading the students' comments, one of the Latina girls spoke up. She started with, I'm actually from Argentina; Mexico is a lot different from Argentina. And the list as you might imagine, went on. I appreciated her openly teaching them about Latino culture. From the frustrated edge in her voice, I was also glad the exchange happened in a relatively safe moderated environment.

I said to the class, It sounds like you might want a few ideas about how to interact or handle the situation. Intercultural relations doesn't mean taking harassment or necessarily being someone's bosom buddy either. It did mean opening up to new ideas and welcoming people.

I told them about my recent trip to Boston where I visited a highly diverse school and how kids hung out together when they found common interests. I asked them if they'd seen teen shows where kids interact from diverse backgrounds. What do you notice they do on the shows? They started coming up with ideas. The students seemed relieved to have a bit of a road map with which to step forward.

A few weeks later I pulled aside the Latino student who I originally noticed receiving the harassment to see if anything had improved since we discussed white-Latino relations. In class they'd turned into great friends, the Latino boy in the middle desk sharing his magazines of flashy cars with the other two white boys oogling with him on either side. Apparently they also high-fived each other in the halls a couple times and who knows what else. This experience led me to believe that focusing on youth, in a moderated safe environment, Utahns and for our discussion, specifically Mormons, make significant improvement interacting in more respectful ways with other races. In fact, I believe that a lot of Mormons in and outside Utah would openly, secretly or even unconsciously hope for moderated modeling to help bridge social and racial gaps.

What seems most unfortunate to me, however, is that so much discussion of race in Utah centers solely around African-Americans, an infinitesimally small number, though growing, mostly in Salt Lake City and a statistically non-existent group in a lot of other areas of Utah. Unless these Utah Mormons individually make regional or global diplomacy decisions in conjunction with African-Americans, they're unlikely to have many opportunities to apply the knowledge. I hope that someday it will become popular to also align the racial and cultural discussion to focus on Latino-Mormon culture which is a much wider need for Utah in many more regions and for every day situations. The education efforts should originate from within Utah where trusted insiders partner with outsiders, Mormon and not, providing Mormons within Utah the same respect people are expecting of them.

Global Mormonism must consider global trends from within the paradigm of individual and regional actors who make choices based on the immediacy of their needs and circumstances. Many Americans and even Mormons who say 'Mormons are racist' imply a broad generalization that excludes the many Mormons of color in the US and around the world who also belong to the vassal state. Is the phrase 'Mormons are racist' actually inherently racist itself as a large and growing percentage of Mormons aren't white? If that phrase is not refering to all Mormons then other Mormons and their biases are excluded from the discussion. Perhaps acknowledgement of a more specific individual and regional analysis of Mormons, including within Utah, will be more revealing.

Hip Hop

I relate to those Provo High students. My first substantial interpersonal encounter with an African American was at twenty-five years of age. By then I had traveled quite a bit. Most of my childhood and young adult years were in Japan and Utah, neither of which had substantial populations of African-Americans. The few African-Americans I met, seemed to assimilate into the larger culture so I had no sense for their concerns or wider culture.

A twenty-something African American drove me to an interpreting assignment where we would be working together. I had just moved to the Washington DC metro area to start my first full time job after grad school. On the way he asked me if I liked Hip Hop. Having never heard of Hip Hop I thought he used it as an adjective, as in, do you like hip hoppy music.

I replied, yes. So he asked me which singers or groups I liked. The list I rattled off was, as you may already realize, not the list he expected. I can't remember how the conversation went exactly because he and I were using common

139

vocabularies to mean totally different things. He started rattling off obscure facts and said I didn't know enough about Black people and how he was very intelligent. I'm not even sure I'm relating the story accurately because I didn't understand at the time why he responded to me the way he did.

I didn't want to admit that most of my knowledge of Black people came from news and TV so to sound a little knowledgeable I brought up the term 'Eubonics' which I now have learned is more officially named AAVE or African American Vernacular English. But that didn't go over well either. I finally revealed that I had just moved from Utah hoping he'd realize that a reasonable person from Utah probably wouldn't know much about African-Americans. He avoided me from then on.

Moments like these made me really nervous talking to African-Americans at first. I heard stories about white people talking about chicken and causing racial tension. Without understanding the context, I thought, if something as normal as eating chicken flared racial tension, I'll avoid any topics but the weather. This fear of naively offending someone prevented me from seeking out interactions with African-Americans.

When I became a teacher at Provo High School a few years later I decided to expose my students to African-Americans. They needed a ready knowledge to prepare themselves for an American culture who expects them to know about African-Americans even if they haven't been exposed to any cultural African-Americans, to witness to the outside world they are open minded and not racist. While I taught at Provo High I took them to Barack Obama's official addresses to students and donated my copy of Obama's biography to the school library.

I briefly met one of the few African Americans I saw in Provo while interpreting an assignment after school hours and immediately invited him as a guest speaker for my American Sign Language classes. I didn't know him but he could sign and would be a natural fit to guest speak for my courses. In reality I didn't care what he would say, I wanted the students to have the exposure to a person with strong black culture.

Turns out he had moved to Utah to avoid the gangs of Los Angeles as I discovered while he was telling stories to the students. The one African-American student in all my classes, totalling about 140 students, seemed to really enjoy listening to him. The speaker carried with him Black culture and pride which African-American students in Provo didn't have ready access. Exposure like this, moderated in a safe environment developed the students' awareness and knowledge base from which to draw when the encounter becomes less structured.

I now understand more about Hip Hop from at least a scholarly perspective. I've learned why the topic of 'chicken' might insight racial tension. My story doesn't represent the experience of all Mormons in Utah but a possibility to what Mormons from Utah may have been exposed. When trying to engage with the African-American community, I find it most helpful to approach it like I would meeting someone in another country because I expect a different culture, withholding assumptions.

I have also come to realize that most African-Americans know as little about my Mormon life and circumstances as I know about them. When African-Americans here in DC respond to me, they often reference the proficiencies of the white people they grew up with or have heard about. Because there isn't a large African American population in Utah, they likely haven't heard much about it except the same kind of rumor and misinformation that I would have heard about them from a distance.

Knowing more about people from Utah might also help African-Americans adjust their expectations of the white people there. A reasonable white person who has grown up on the east coast for example should have a certain base of knowledge about African Americans and Black people in general. A Chinese person in China probably would not. I have met Black people who related their interactions with Chinese people who say all sorts of funny things on their first encounter with a Black person, some of which could be considered racially charged. However, the Black person I spoke with chuckled and rolled their eyes and took it as an opportunity to educate. There is little to no expectation that a Chinese person in China would know anything about Black people but what they've seen on the news. Perhaps African-Americans might be willing to adjust their expectations for Mormons in Utah in the same vein. African Americans and Mormon Utah might be better served approaching the Mormon/African-American dynamic as an international relations issue rather than from an American minority one.

Utah can be desceptive, however. If a Utah Mormon served a mission to a location heavily populated with Black people, they might know more than the average white American, embrace African-American values and exhibit cultural expertise. Any reasonable white Utah Mormon, though, is expected to know a few phrases in Spanish. They are also learning holidays, important Latino coming of age rights, expectations, and manners.

Being generationally Mormon in any country can be as much a social boundary or border as it is religious. I have found that Americans in much of the rest of the United States have similar ideals and goals as Mormons but use different terminology, approaches, and methods to reach them. Mormons are a bit foreign; we may speak the same language but the cultures are different enough to acknowledge outsiders may need a guide book and a short dictionary of terms. Individual Mormons are as much or even more influenced by Mormon social dimensions as American ones. The same applies to Mormons in other parts of the world. It's like holding two passports. Mormons from Utah, though are less likely to speak both languages, native Mormon and fluent American.

Practicalities

Let's look for some of these famed American of American Mormons, those who joined the church as Americans and moved across the plains, like so many stories tell us, to Utah. I thought for sure one of my good friends would fit the bill. She is another friend I met in Jerusalem on a study abroad but she always loved her farm town in the United States. Later in grad school my European roommates in England all thought she was very American, too.

Nellene Howard Stevens is generationally Mormon from Blackfoot, Idaho. She took me once to the wide open fields of her hometown about three driving hours from an airport. The air was clean, the night sky prickled with dusty shimmer. She could name all the geologies of the rocks in the field across from her family's house. She chuckled at memories of her friends playing in the deep irrigation ditch a few minutes away. She took me to rodeos and car smashing exhibitions in wide open rural towns. She's also taken advantage of all sorts of travel excursions to Jerusalem, to Japan on a Mormon mission, Africa, and several other US domestic and international locations. One of her

neighbors a few large blocks away housed
Japanese exchange students and spoke Japanese.
They're just the type of down to earth people you
hope still exist in the world.

So I asked her, where are your ancestors
from? She might just be one of those famous
American-born converts to Mormonism.

I'm mostly English, she replied. They
converted in England.

Mostly? What about the others who are
not English?

Oh right. They're Irish and Scottish.

Goodness, I thought. Even the rodeo
cowgirl lover is not originally American before her
family was Mormon.

Maybe that's why I grew up so obsessed
with England, she said. Perhaps. Hmmm.

But where can we find one of these
American of Americans, the ones actors blow a
lung on Broadway about, the New Englanders who
disapeared to Utah? I actually did meet one once,
though I don't believe he is bigoted. He was
actually working, a chamelion practically, in
Washington DC.

I began asking Mormons where their geneology came from and when their family converted. It's a dangerous occupation, by the way, but it's terribly interesting. One night at our dinner table a guest pulled out of his wallet a pedigree chart, I kid you not. The entire chart was American going back to the Massachusetts Bay Company. There was a sole European on the entire chart. Who do you suppose this American of American Mormons was related to? Prophet-presidents and top leaders of the church all the way to the Smith line, though I believe it was Joseph Smith's brother Hyrum. Then Joseph and Hyrum Smith were related to early presidents of the United States. Is there anyone more American that that?

These American-Americans are so rare you almost want to put them in a museum. They're the only ones left, quickly becoming extinct, that could clearly make the case for an all-American religion. Everyone else is not American-American, they're Mormon.

I know Mormons who've forgotten that they are themselves foreigners in many ways, causing a storm of bitterness and xenophobia for others. These Mormons make the news and the blogs. There are grubby Mormon power mongers who play socialist at church, then dishonestly lobby for wealth and position the other six days of the week. I'm not sure what to do with determined rascals and bitter diatribes, actually. Are these real Mormons? Have I luckily averted their corupt influence, for the most part, my whole Mormon life? How do we really know who are the real Mormons or are Mormons actually diverse within the vassal state? But let's say I'm not seeing something that other people are seeing. After all the top fifteen leaders are almost all American so that lack of diversity, however originated, must represent a sentiment somewhere.

Suppose, however, that there are more pedestrian reasons for an international body as a vassal state to continue sustaining American leaders. While it is impossible to know for sure, hypothesizing may at least open us to possibilities we might not have explored.

For one, because the Mormon vassal state at headquarters answers to the US government, the right to stay in Salt Lake City for long periods of time requires US government approval, a green card at the very least. Citizenship at best. An apostle in the top fifteen of Mormon leadership at this point in time requires permanent residence in Utah. But even more than that, a US passport. Green card holders are not entitled to US passports and most other passports do not have the range of travel options that a US passport ensures. That limits a potentially international Mormon apostle in two ways. One, they would need to become a US citizen which may take at least five years and possibly longer. Two, if they weren't a US citizen, their passport would limit the range of their travel and access particularly to the US itself.

Imagine, though, for a minute that Mormons called an apostle permanently stationed in the UK precluding the necessity of US citizenship who met with senior leadership over video conference for minor meetings and flew in for major meetings. A UK passport is also expansive and perhaps would open new territories that a US passport does not. Would that be much different than the current European apostle in the top fifteen, Elder Dieter Uchtdorf from Germany who resides in Utah? It would have a different feel and Britons would have to stop mocking the accents, if that is possible. The UK may not be the diversity people hoped for, however. Another feasible option may still surface but the list of viable options for globe traveling leaders is constrained. A Mormon of color who is also an American or UK citizen is the obvious alternative for the near term if following an American style of diversity is the best new course of action.

So if the Mormon vassal state is centered in Utah, foreign-born immigrants and their descendents might explain several phenomina:

149

divergence of Mormon Utah from the wider American culture, Mormons who weren't actually all Americans moving west, xenophobia for even other white Americans with whom they never had to fully integrate to the same extent as say an immigrant to New York, etc.

What it doesn't seem to explain, though, is why Mormons who with a heavily foreign-born population in Utah didn't appoint foreign-born apostles in their top fifteen leadership from nearly the beginning. At that point, citizenship and passport issues were not as vital because they could draw on the foreign-born within Utah. Managing thousands of new immigrants streaming into Utah seems to demand at least a couple foreign-born leaders to facilitate integration, does it not?

But as a vassal state, American-born leaders do make a lot of sense. With a tenuous relationship with the host nation (the US), appearing as American and patriotic as possible likely served two purposes. One, to mollify a government who not only threatened but actually sent troops against Mormons. Federal officials stationed in Utah jailed Mormons for practicing polygamy and took away their suffrage. Two, when thousands upon thousands of new immigrants showed up, encouraging a shared identity of 'Americanness' facilitated a goal of federal statehood within the US to not only encourage integration but also economic connectivity with the east coast. American leaders facilitated an American façade for expediency in a country where whiteness and Americanness mattered at the time.

International site-based religions are all in a unique position. Catholics headquarter their pope in his own nation-state of the Vatican city with control over passports. Judaism tenuously controls its borders in Jerusalem and Tel Aviv, though there is no central leadership. Diversity within Israel proper versus diversity within a narrow range of fifteen is more the concern. Islam controls many of its religious sites though not all. There is a unique dynamic for pilgrims traveling to the Hajj regarding passports and permits. Though, again, Islam does not have one centralized leadership body. Hindus and other eastern religions are similar to Islam regarding passports and central leadership.

Mormons as a religion are not in control of Utah. They operate somewhat independently but are still contrained by US and Utah state law. What happens, though, if Americans once again turn against Mormons? A majority American leadership at the top of the Mormon vassal state mitigating these issues may still be a practicality. A foreign-born leader is great. Perhaps more people of color even if American-born may become an eventual reality.

But what if my sample size for evaluating Mormons is too small? What if my own familiarity among Mormons in Japan, in the university inculcated town of Provo, the Mormons in Taibei, the diversity of backgrounds of Mormons in Bangkok, London, Jerusalem, and Cairo don't represent the essense of who Mormons are? Perhaps the farmers and businessmen in the beautiful town of Blackfoot, Idaho are the real Mormons and city dweller Mormons are the fringe. I wouldn't mind that either. The beauty is that Blackfoot Mormons are just as representative as all the other locations' Mormons.

Admittance

Lastly, have you ever wondered why Mormons don't hammer down a sign on their church building's lawn proclaiming the Sunday sermon inviting all to attend? Closed and locked doors except during services and activities are the norm. Perhaps because Mormons are unpaid, they need to speed back to their day jobs.

Most often if someone visits a Mormon Sunday service, they arrive with a couple of snappy dressed missionaries wearing identifying tags. To become Mormon, no matter how many years a person has been hanging with their Mormon buddies, they have to meet with missionaries for a set of lessons. Then there is an interview with questions and then you get approval for baptism. This appears less inviting than a few of my Protestant friends' church meetings I've witnessed. Yet, this somewhat resembles the citizenship process of a nation-state as we have said before. To become a citizen of a country, you pledge certain things and renounce others. Becoming Mormon is like receiving dual citizenship. One Mormon code is to sustain, honor and obey the government under which you live. You are still the citizen of whatever culture or nationality you belong to but you are also now a citizen of the Mormon vassal state with fellow citizens living all over the world. Diversity happens with dual citizenships, Mormon and something else.

Why, though, do we not hear the international story of Mormons more consistently? My hypothesis is that most Mormon decision makers were American-born Mormons and their descendents. Writers and artists emphasized the American story partially because that is the paradigm in which they grew up. If your great great grandfather made a decision that impacted people, you are more likely to take the time to write about it or paint a picture of the scene. You are also more likely to write about Mormons if you're disenchanted over policies and behaviors. Mormon authorities also censored writings fearful of damaging the delicate relationship with the US, or, many believe, they wanted to get rid of undesirables. Perhaps, depending on the person and the situation, both reasons are true. The archives are now open. The internet prevents official censorship. Stories are now surfacing.

When we're satisfied with the status quo we have much more pressing matters to address like the bills or the leaky sink. We're far more likely to write a journal entry at the end of the day for future posterity than write a book for strangers to read. The books we read, by whoever took the time to write them, influence how we view the variables around us, but they may not be the whole story. I believe there is and always has been an even more compelling international story of Mormonism. It just needs to be written.

Adopting the Best

Mormonism may not be an actual vassal state in an official legal sense. The comparison, though, helps us analyze Mormons within different paradigms, to not assume that Mormons should or will behave like other Americans in the United States; to ask new questions, to find new solutions. When the international body desires an international leader at its helm or even an American or Briton of color, perhaps speaking Mormon, or using the frame that contrains Mormons to discuss and request this goal will be more effective than using the more foreign Western Liberal verbage to achieve these ends.

Drawing from the best of Western thought and liberal principles I want to infuse my Mormon values of diversity. Recognizing distinct variables only present in the Mormon context I favor a dual passport, Mormon-unique global vassal state.

Author & Other Titles

The Writer's Digest 75th Annual Writing Competition awarded AA Bastian an Honorable Mention in the Memoirs/Personal Essay category for "Japanese Carp", a critical look at childhood as a military dependent in Okinawa. She also serves as an editor for the Washington Independent Review of Books.

She's working on a history of a Connecticut man who becomes Mormon and is sent on a mission to Siam in the 1850s. She taught American Sign Language and Arabic in high school and is currently a full time writer, interpreter and business owner living and working in the Washington DC metro area.

Other books:

Baggage on the Hooghly: Race, Asia, and the Mormons

Boots in the Temple: A Collection

www.ingramcontent.com/pod-product-compliance
Lightning Source LLC
Chambersburg PA
CBHW050449290526
45786CB00006B/2224